# Finding Hidden Voices of the Chinese Railroad Workers

## An Archaeological and Historical Journey

Mary L. Maniery, Rebecca Allen, and Sarah Christine Heffner

I0528552

**SOCIETY** *for*
**HISTORICAL**
**ARCHAEOLOGY**

The Society for Historical Archaeology
Special Publication Series No. 13
2016

In association with the

**CHINESE**
**HISTORICAL**
**SOCIETY** OF
**AMERICA**

ChineseRailroadWorkers 北美鐵路華工研究工程
*in North America Project* at Stanford University 項目組

**Finding Hidden Voices of the Chinese Railroad Workers**
**An Archaeological and Historical Journey**

Library of Congress Control Number 2016933967

Authors: Mary L. Maniery, Rebecca Allen, and Sarah Christine Heffner

Contributors: Gordon H. Chang, Sue Fawn Chung, John Joseph Crandall, Kelly J. Dixon, Shelley Fisher Fishkin, Sue Lee, Chris Merritt, Michael R. Polk, Amber Rankin, Timothy R. Urbaniak, Barbara L. Voss, and Connie Young Yu.

Cover photo by Adrianna Allen
Back cover photo by Adrianna Allen (graffiti in Donner Summit Tunnel)
Historic photo: Tea carrier heading east from the opening of Tunnel No. 8, Donner Summit.
(Photo by Alfred Hart, Library of Congress, LC-USZ62-50457)

Richard Schaefer, Copy Editor
Camille Majors, Book Designer

Printed in the United States of America

Annalies Corbin, Co-Publications Editor

*Dedicated to Chinese railroad workers,*
*the backbone of the transcontinental railroad.*

# Contents

# The Strength of Collaboration
## —Annalies Corbin, SHA Co-Publications Editor

Formed in 1967, the Society for Historical Archaeology is the largest international scholarly group concerned with the archaeology of the modern world (A.D. 1400–present). Our society promotes scholarly research and the dissemination of knowledge concerning historical archaeology. We are specifically concerned with the identification, excavation, interpretation, and conservation of sites and materials on land and underwater.

One of the society's primary goals is to educate and share with the public the findings of our research. This volume represents a collaboration of organizations and individuals to do just that. I would like to extend a personal thank you, on behalf of the Society for Historical Archaeology, to the following groups that worked with the authors to tell the extraordinary story of the Chinese railroad workers.

*Chinese Historical Society of America*

*Chinese Railroad Workers in North America Project at Stanford University*

*Environmental Science Associates*

*PAR Environmental Services, Inc.*

# Why Archaeology?

### —Rebecca Allen and Mary Maniery

Historians look to papers and books to reconstruct the past. Archaeologists find clues in the bits and fragments of everyday life. Combining archaeological evidence with existing documents offers an expanded view of Chinese railroad-worker history. As historical archaeologists, we use both sources to ask new questions of old documents and challenge previous histories. Our goal is to offer new interpretations and add depth to the understanding of the past.

In the late 19th century, the United States sought to establish control of western lands and natural resources. The West was a land of small, isolated communities scattered across a vast landscape. Construction of a transcontinental railroad promised a way to link established cities and markets east of the Mississippi River with the growing patchwork of settlements of the West. This vision would require engineering, large investments of capital, legislative support, and a massive labor force. The completion of this railroad across western lands in 1869 was among the most significant and far-reaching events in our nation's history.

Railroad histories often relegate the Chinese to a footnote, acknowledging their necessity for railroad construction, but offering few details about the workers themselves. In large part this is probably because they left no written history behind (at least not that has been identified to date). Another factor contributing to the anonymity of the labor force was the organization of the workers themselves. Many railroad payroll records carefully listed the names and jobs of their employees. Most Chinese worked for labor contractors in groups of 20–30 men, with one person acting as company liaison with the railroad. While the Quang Leung Company may be listed in the records, the 30 men that Quang Leung represented remain nameless, among thousands of the hidden voices that were crucial to the successful completion of the railroad.

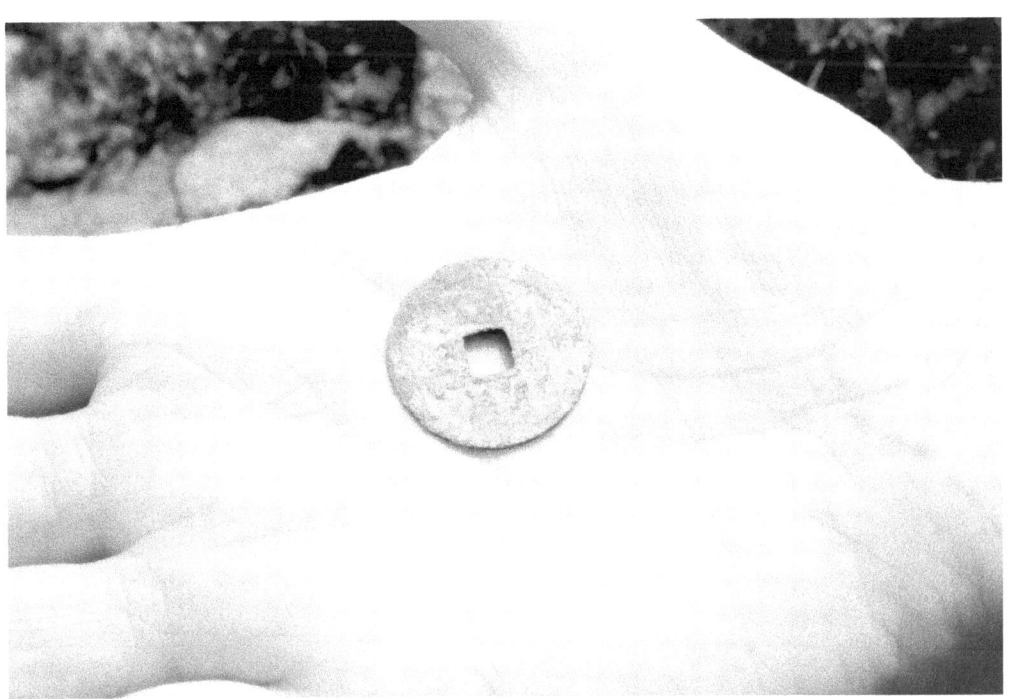

*The history of the Chinese pioneers and builders of the West is still hidden in an occasional sentence and obscure paragraph in the dusty and forgotten old books of the last century. These bits of the past can be found only by an endless search through these lost books. Having searched through hundreds, perhaps thousands, I know.*

### —Stan Steiner, historian, 1979

As researchers, a frustrating barrier for writing about this period is that historical lithographs, illustrations, and newspaper accounts do not display the range of ages, dress, and activities of Chinese laborers that we see reflected in the archaeological record. From our perspective, many historical images depict stereotypes and sometimes caricatures, and often show a narrow vision of the life and experiences of the workers. Through our research we tried to find illustrations that provide a more accurate and specific image of the camps. We also wanted to make the book and its concepts accessible to a diverse audience through a vibrantly illustrated format. We worked with historical illustrations, archaeological evidence, and photographs of the modern landscape that include remnants of the past (see appendix for all illustration captions and credits). We also engaged the assistance of a graphic artist, who in her day job works with archaeologists, and at the same time is enrolled as an art student, learning animated illustration. All these sources helped us to envision the past.

The Chinese who labored on the transcontinental railroad brought their own vision of their economic and social place on the railroad-construction force, but factors beyond their control often dictated their daily lives. The physical evidence of their everyday lives provides a quiet reminder of the necessary adjustments made to thrive in a new country, alien environment, and physically challenging work. The evidence adds a broader picture, one that highlights choices and occurrences that were part of their set routine. This teasing-out of information is the sleuthing of archaeologists, who use fragments of the past to interpret the Chinese experience in new ways, to amplify the muted voices of the past, and to better understand the challenges and discrimination that the workers faced, as well as the problems they solved to make new environments manageable. Together, archaeological and historical evidence suggests that, regardless of their circumstances, the Chinese who worked on the railroad had an active role in shaping national history.

# Artist's Preface

## —Amber Rankin

I began constructing the drawings found in this book by using the historical lithographs and photos provided by Mary, Rebecca, and Sarah. These images served as the basis of each scene, helped to develop a setting, and served as a jumping-off point for additional research. For the past five years, I have worked as a graphic artist for PAR Environmental Services, Inc., where I create and digitize archaeological field maps and illustrate important artifacts. As an artist I have always had a deep love of history, both in my work at PAR and in the development of my graduate thesis. My background in both archaeological technical illustration and animation gave me a unique perspective on this project that went beyond simply recreating historical illustrations and allowed me to reimagine individuals that would be accessible to a wide modern audience.

From these images I began to work on creating more unique individuals, at first using historical photographs of camps and other similar settings from the time period to establish proper posing and clothing choices. In these photos, the workers' faces were often obscured or unreadable and, so, to further bring my characters to life, I turned to San Francisco immigration photos, and also photos from the Jiangmen Wuyi Musem of Overseas Chinese in Guangdong, China, sent to us by our colleagues. I chose specific images to serve as a reference for each character in order to avoid generalization in the final drawing. My animation background led me to develop scenes that focused on characters, thoughts, and motivations, so that characters are specific people in a time and place. I imagined exhausted workers relaxing with an evening meal at their campsite, grooming themselves, or enjoying the challenge of gambling. At the same time, I was influenced by photographs of Chinese workers in European American dress. I sought to create well-rounded personalities, representing a wide range of character traits and attitudes. I wanted to create memorable characters with which readers could engage and identify.

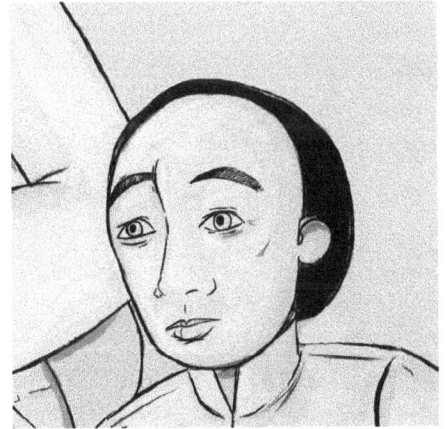

# 1
# Building the Railroad

Building the Railroad

Adapting to a New Environment

Defining Identity

Health and Well-Being

Leisure

Leaving a Legacy

Appendices

# Beginnings

In 1966–1967 two young archaeologists working in the high country of California's Sierra Nevada range came across a series of sites marked by stone foundations, bits of cans, and piles of ceramic pieces. Their identification of these Chinese-occupied construction camps and subsequent reporting of their find at the 1969 Society for Historical Archaeology national meeting sparked an interest in the archaeology of the Chinese who came to America that continues today. Over the last 50 years archaeologists have studied sites occupied by Chinese miners, loggers, charcoal makers, and railroad workers. Towns, laundries, cobbler shops, merchant establishments, places of worship, and recreation and association halls have been excavated and studied. Similar work camps, also occupied by Chinese, have been found and studied in Canada, Australia, and New Zealand.

Many Chinese came to the United States before the building of the transcontinental railroad. These immigrants primarily came as miners or merchants, arriving individually or in small groups. They faced discrimination and racial hatred, but many stayed. Working for the railroad offered new opportunities.

In contrast, those who came from China specifically to build the railroad were recruited by the thousands and transported in large groups to the United States.

It took engineering foresight to see the possibilities of a railroad crossing the country and to plot a route. It took capitalists with enough financial and political clout to turn that possibility into a reality. Finally, it took a business owner who recognized that the answer to California's labor shortage lay across the ocean to the west, rather than toward the traditional employment centers of the East, and who figured out how to get the labor needed in spite of prejudice, distance, and language barriers. Our story begins with these visionaries who set the stage for what became one of the largest building efforts in United States history, and then turns to exploring the daily life of the laborers who provided the blood and sweat to make the vision a success. Today, archaeologists have returned to that high country and locations beyond, tracing the steps of the Chinese workers, and finding more evidence of their struggle, with the goal of keeping the knowledge of their achievements alive for future generations.

# The Engineer's Vision and the Business of the Railroad

**Theodore Dehone Judah** came to California as a young railroad engineer in 1854. He was hired to build the Sacramento Valley Railroad (SVRR), the first railroad west of the Mississippi River. Even while building the SVRR, Judah dreamed of a railroad that would link the East and West coasts of America and unite the country. He surveyed a viable route across the Sierra Nevada mountain range, and convinced a group of businessmen to invest in his route. Judah sold the concept and feasibility of the route to politicians in Washington, D.C. He made three trips back East, carrying his survey maps, reports, and draft legislative bills, convincing the legislators that his dream could become a reality. He succeeded.

**Leland Stanford** served as president of the Central Pacific Railroad. A lawyer by training, he was a tremendously powerful man and an eloquent speaker. His became the face of the Central Pacific, and his passionate pro-railroad speeches, while a state senator and as a former governor of California, garnered much support for the railroad.

*Everything he did from the time he went to California to the day of his death was for the great continental Pacific railway. Time, money, brains, strength, body and soul were absorbed. It was the burden of his thought day and night.*

—*Mrs. Anna Judah, Memoirs, about 1863*

**Collis Potter Huntington** took on the role of vice president for the Central Pacific. His business sense was crucial in achieving the Railroad's goals.

**Mark Hopkins** served as company treasurer and was known for his thriftiness. It was said that he knew how to squeeze 106¢ out of every dollar, a much-needed trait for the successful building of the railroad.

**Charles Crocker**, chief of construction, was the labor manager and construction genius. Recognizing that the labor pool in California was inadequate, he is credited with hiring Chinese as workers. It was an uphill battle to convince his partners that Chinese laborers could do the job, and he faced strong racial prejudice from his partners, crew supervisors, and the public. Despite the opposition, Crocker recruited Chinese workers in California and in China, gaining a labor force of thousands and proving that his belief in the Chinese was well founded.

# Bridging the Gap

During the Civil War railroad development in the eastern third of the United States accelerated to support both sides of the war effort. By 1865, the eastern U.S. was crisscrossed with rails, while the majority of the country, from Omaha to Sacramento, relied on a few wagon roads. Crossing the country was a trip that took months.

Two companies built the transcontinental railroad. The Union Pacific Railroad began at Omaha, building west across the Great Plains. The Central Pacific's route started at Sacramento and headed east, crossing the Sierra Nevada mountains and the barren deserts of Nevada. The two companies united their individual lines at Promontory Point, Utah, years after construction began, finally bridging the gap between the eastern seaboard and the Pacific west.

Promontory Point

Omaha

Sacramento

- – – Central Pacific Railroad
- ▪ – ▪ Union Pacific Railroad

As the Civil War ended, both Union and Confederate soldiers, released from duty and seeking employment, drifted west and provided the Union Pacific with a ready supply of laborers. The Union Pacific labor force was completed with the addition of Irish-immigrant workers from the eastern cities, African Americans (including those formerly enslaved), and, as the route neared Promontory Point, Mormon and Native American workers.

Finding a labor force was much harder out west. Faced with the daunting task of blasting a path through the high mountains separating California and Nevada, and then crossing the hot desert, the Central Pacific's solution was to look to the Chinese as reliable hard workers. At first, Crocker drew on the many Chinese already in California. As the local labor pool was exhausted, Crocker worked with labor contractors to bring more workers directly from China.

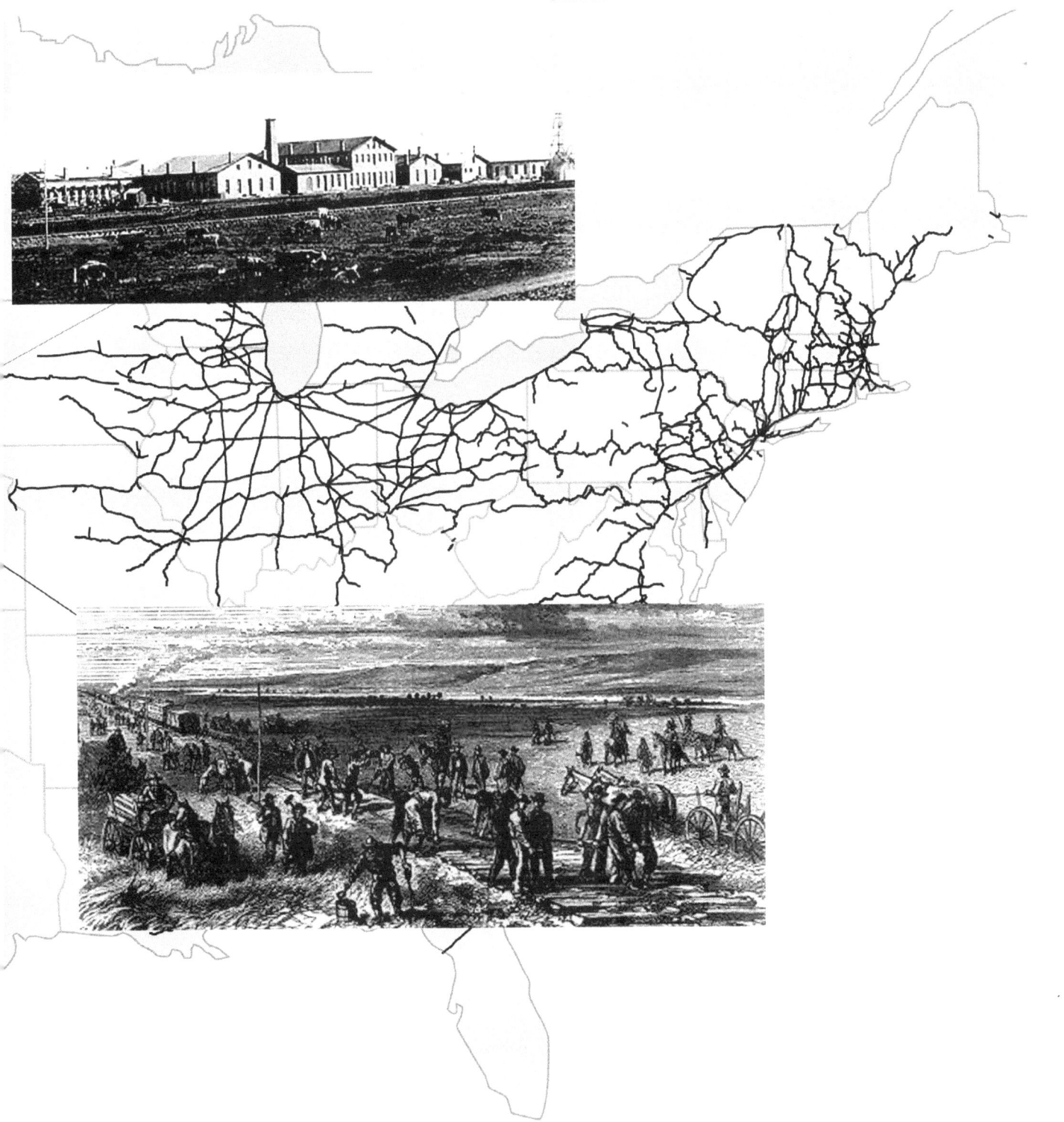

# Recruiting the Crews

*Did they not build the Chinese Wall, the biggest piece of masonry in the world?*

—Charles Crocker, Central Pacific Chief of Construction, 1865

When Crocker focused his recruiting efforts on China, he found a people up to the challenge. Guangdong Province in southeast China had experienced many years of hardship. People living in the area were heavily taxed. Civil war, floods, and other natural disasters only added to the extreme poverty of the region. In addition to the internal pressure, external conditions were unfavorable as Western powers attempted to carve China into their own sphere of interest and undermine its economy. Many Chinese were ready to brave a new country in order to support their families.

Crocker hired independent businesses, such as Sisson, Wallace & Co., to recruit workers from China. Those companies negotiated with representatives from regions of Guangdong to persuade their fellow countrymen in China that California would welcome their labor.

Labor contractors lent each man the cost of passage to California and guaranteed him work. It took about two-and-a-half years to pay off the cost of passage.

CHINA

RAILROAD GAZETTEER.        53

## SISSON, WALLACE & CO.

GENERAL AGENTS FOR

## CHINESE LABOR,

Wholesale and Retail Dealers in

## Chinese Goods,

GROCERIES,

*PROVISIONS, LIQUORS, CLOTHING,*

Hardware, Produce, Grain,

**And all kinds of Family Supplies.**

Well appointed Stores located on lines of Western Pacific, California and Oregon, and Central Pacific Railroads at

*Pleasanton,        Chico,        Truckee,*
*Winnemucca,        Carlin,        Toano,*
*and Corinne.*

We have furnished, and continue to furnish above Railroads with CHINESE LABOR, and are fully prepared to fill orders for this class of labor, in any part of the country.

Principal Office, No. 12 J Street, Sacramento.
*San Francisco Office, No. 228 Clay St.*

Ships heading overseas left from Canton, Macao, or Hong Kong. To get to California, workers were crammed onto any available ship leaving from these ports.

Life onboard ship was similar to their future lives in the railroad camps. The men were divided by their county of origin into groups of 12–30. Each group had one spokesman who was responsible for procuring food and supplies and then distributing them to the group.

# By the Sweat of Their Brows

The majority of the Chinese employed by the Central Pacific were laborers. Divided into small groups of about 12–30, they served as construction vanguards, preparing the grade by breaking up rocks, shoveling dirt to form cuts, or piling up soil for fill areas. Other teams of workers followed behind once the track and trails were laid, pounding in spikes and finishing up the grade.

To this day no one knows exactly how many Chinese the Central Pacific employed. Scholars have poured over the payroll records, counting the numbers of "companies" and estimating the labor-force numbers based on simple math: the number of companies listed in the records multiplied by 20 each. Crocker estimated that, at the peak of construction, about 10,000 Chinese workers toiled on the railroad. Some historians argue that the number was closer to 14,000, while others suggest that the peak labor force included up to 23,000 workers. No matter the number, scholars now recognize that the sweat, blood, and labor of the Chinese workers were the backbone of the construction effort.

CENTRAL PACIFIC RAILROAD—CHINESE LABORERS AT WORK.

*Systematic workers these Chinese—competent and wonderfully effective. ... Divided into gangs of about 30 men each, they work under the direction of an American foreman. The Chinese board themselves. One of their number is selected in each gang to receive all wages and buy all provisions. They usually pay an American clerk—$1 a month apiece is usual—to see that each gets all he earned and is charged no more than his share of the living expenses. They are paid from $30 to $35 in gold a month, out of which they board themselves. They are credited with having saved about $20 a month. Their workday is from sunrise to sunset, six days in the week.*

—*Alta California, September 9, 1868*

*A large part of our force are Chinese. ... We are training them to all kinds of labor blasting, driving horses, handling rock, as well as the pick and shovel.*

—*E. B. Crocker, Central Pacific Legal Counsel, to friend Cornelius Cole, April 1865*

*Many of them are becoming very expert in drilling, blasting, and other departments of rock work.*

—*Samuel S. Montague, Central Pacific Chief Engineer, 1865*

## *Tools of the Trade*

Archaeologists often find discarded tools and railroad-related artifacts at Chinese work camps along the railroad. The Central Pacific provided the tools of the trade to the laborers. Photographic images of workers taken during construction show shovels, sledgehammers, and picks to break up rocks, and drill bits used for making holes to insert dynamite for blasting outcrops.

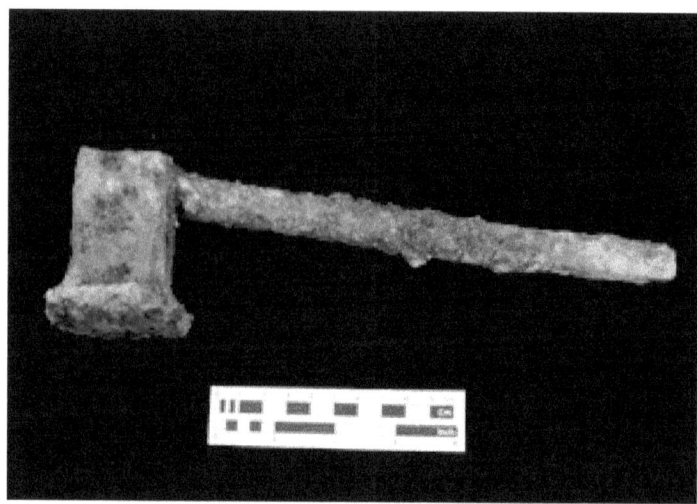

Short-handled sledgehammers were a necessary part of the blacksmith's toolkit. Laborers used long-handled sledges to break up rock and pound in spikes.

Workers used files to sharpen the shovels, picks, axes, and other tools.

While wooden handles are rarely preserved, the steel blades of shovels are often found at work-camp sites, such as this example from a railroad construction camp site high up in the Sierra Nevada range. Many were used until most of the blade was worn away.

Along with tools, camps often contain bits and pieces of railroad equipment, such as the ubiquitous spikes shown here, and links and pins used to connect rail cars.

This Central Pacific Railroad (CPRR) padlock was used to lock up engines, equipment, and other supplies along the railroad.

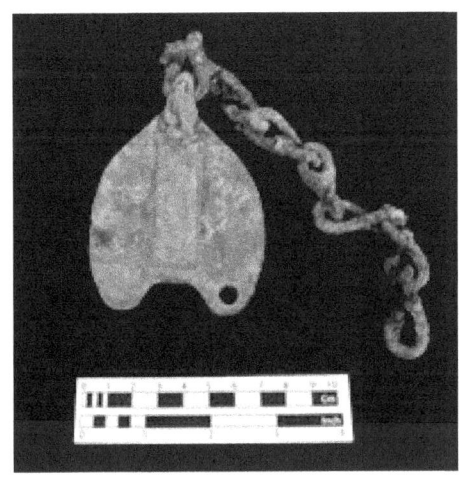

## The Donner Summit Tunnels

The Donner Summit tunnels in California are perhaps the most famous accomplishment of the Chinese railroad workers. At high elevation and during inclement weather, workers blasted and excavated a series of seven tunnels within the space of two miles. Excavated from four directions, Tunnel No. 6 was the longest at 1,659 ft., dug 124 ft. beneath a surface of solid granite with a 30 ft. change in elevation. Laborers tunneled into the granite face and created occasional air shafts by placing black-powder charges to blast the rock free. Another crew removed the loosened rock after each explosion. The accomplishment of creating this series of tunnels took four long years of hard work, from 1865 to 1869. Work went on year-round, sometimes with more than 40 ft. of snow on the ground in the winter.

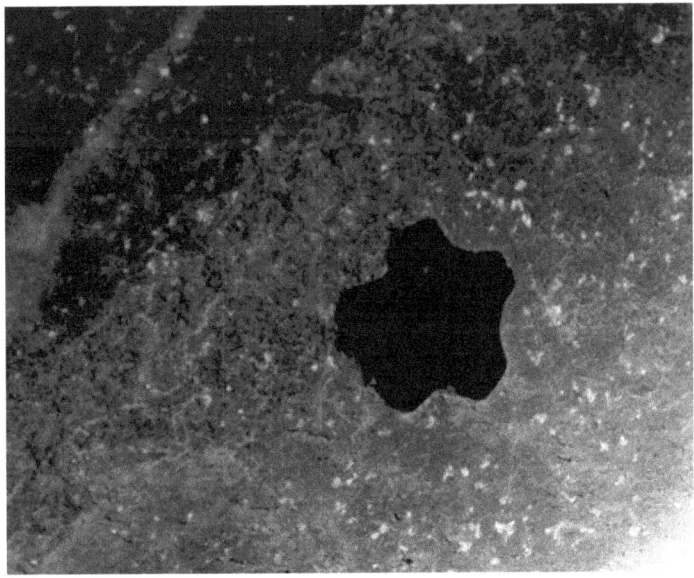

From a scenic pullout along U.S. Highway 40, visitors can still see the route of the transcontinental railroad, nestled along the granite outcrops. Today, modern concrete snow sheds built between the tunnels are more visible, but the route is the same. Portions of the Donner Summit tunnels are accessible to hikers. With a good flashlight in hand, hikers can see the amazing results of Chinese workers' labors: the hand-excavated rock face of the tunnel, scars from drilling rods, metal rods and brackets hammered into the granite wall, and abandoned railroad ties. Graffiti now covers much of the concrete snow-shed forms; at least one artist has left poignant reminders of the Chinese railroad workers at the junctures where concrete walls adjoin the hand-hewn tunnels. The last train went through this tunnel in 1993.

## The Indispensable Help

Railroad camps usually were segregated by race, ethnicity, or job tasks, and Chinese workers generally lived apart from their non-Chinese counterparts. While most Chinese worked as laborers, close study of payroll records indicates that some Chinese also worked in non-Chinese camps, doing such tasks as cooking or waiting tables. At these camps, Chinese occupations are listed as "Cook," "Night Cook," or "Waiter." Camp No. 51, one of the larger non-Chinese camps, operated with the help of 12 Chinese waiters, a night cook, two blacksmith helpers, and several laborers.

Camp No. *28*

C. P.

PAY ROLL No. *999* , fo[r]

Received from C. CROCKER, Contractor, Central

names, for services performed during the month of *July*

| NAMES. | OCCUPATION | No. of Days | Rate per Diem. |
|---|---|---|---|
| Chas E Thomas | Foreman | 26 | |
| R Vanverde | Cook | 31 | |
| Ah Jung | 2d Cook | 14 | 66 |
| Ah John | " | 6 | 66 |
| Ah Sin | " | 9 | 66 |
| G W Mc Adams | Blacksmith 15. Blacksmiths | 16 | 250 239 |
| John Jay | Helper 16. ... | 31 | 134 |
| Ah Git | Blacksmith | 27½ | 153 |
| Ah Sin | Helper | 26½ | 100 |
| Ah Wen | Helper | 15 | 100 |
| John Kennedy | Hostler | 31 | |

Other Chinese men chopped wood or acted as blacksmith "helpers." One man, Ah Gib, is listed as the blacksmith for Camp No. 28 and had two of his countrymen working alongside him as assistants.

A few men worked as grooms, or hostlers, charged with taking care of the horses used to pull wagons and equipment.

# 2
# Adapting to a New Environment

## New Landscapes

Most Chinese workers came from small villages in Guangdong's Pearl River delta, a low-lying area full of ponds, rivers, and lush vegetation. Long, hot, wet summers and short, mild winters characterize the region's climate.

While Chinese labored throughout the western U.S., perhaps the most extreme conditions they faced were in the Sierra Nevada mountains and the Nevada desert. This is a land of granite and pines, steep terrain, seas of sand, and rapidly changing climate— from extreme heat to extreme cold. To survive in this new environment, workers had to adapt.

# The Camps

After arriving in San Francisco some workers were whisked directly to the camps. Others headed up river to Sacramento, the western terminus of the Central Pacific. When Chinese immigrants arrived in Sacramento (via San Francisco), they sought temporary housing in the established "Chinatown" on I Street or in boats moored in the river opposite the railyard. This Sacramento community was the starting point for many of the railroad workers, housing them overnight and providing them with supplies before they headed east into the mountains.

Housing for workers along the construction route was supplied partially by the Central Pacific and supplemented by the employees. From boats to tents to cabins and boxcars, the workers experienced a variety of camp conditions. From extreme cold to extreme heat, the workers did their best to make a home out of what the railroad company offered them.

After 150 years, the now-forgotten locations of camps are often marked by subtle changes on the landscape. Shallow depressions indicate the dugouts where Chinese laborers slept. A leveled tent pad, alignment of rocks, bits of glass and dishes glittering in the sand, railroad spikes, and other traces of the past are clues for which archaeologists search, as they work to identify the long-lost camps of the railroad workers.

*By the side of the grade smokes the camp fires of the blue clad laborers who could be seen in groups waiting for the signal to start work. These are the Chinese, and the job ... is to clear a level roadbed for the track. Miles back is the camp of the rear guard—the Chinese who follow the track gang, ballasting and finishing the roadbed.*

—*Alta California, November 9, 1868*

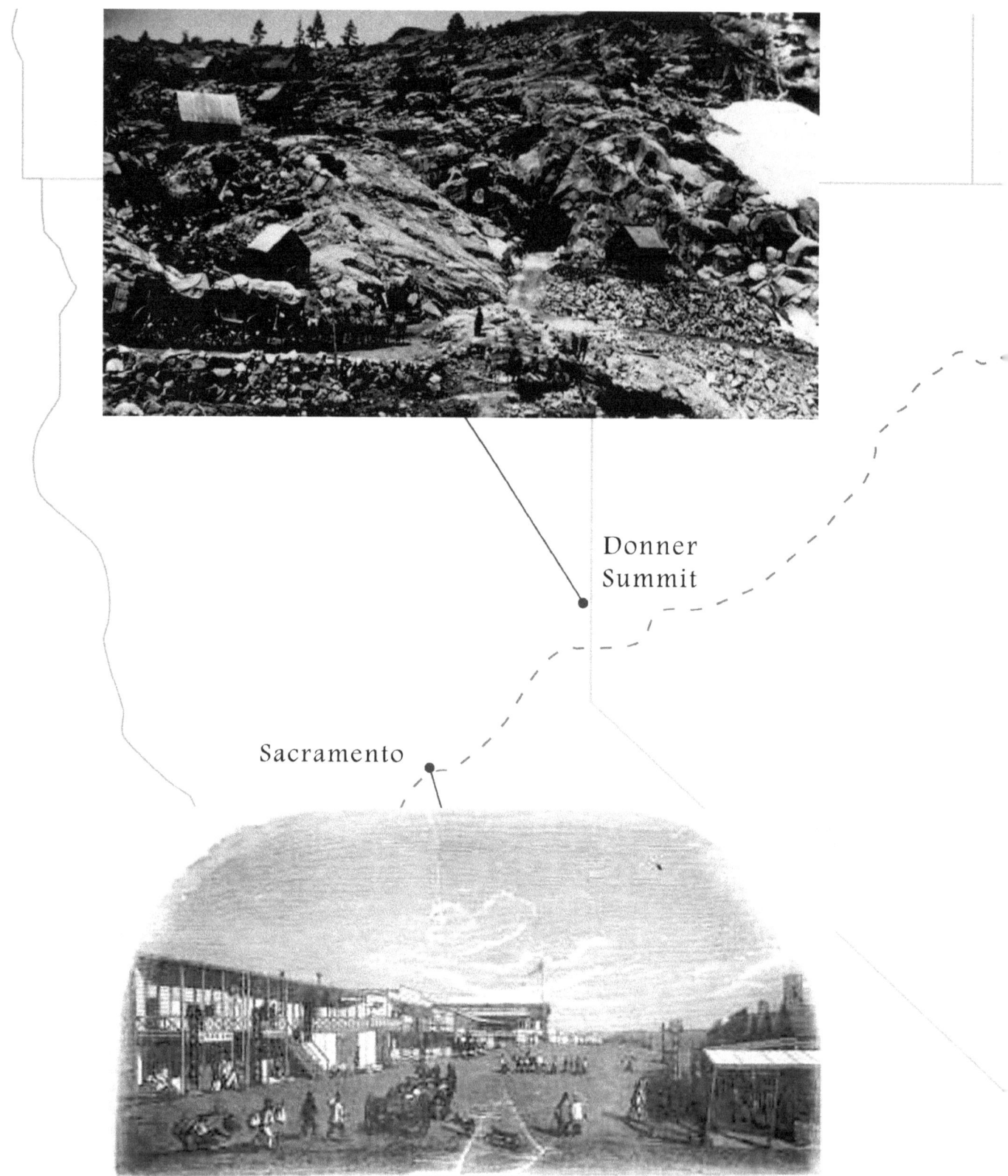

Donner Summit

Sacramento

## Changing Shelters

As construction slowed down in the high Sierra, it became apparent that, in the winter months, cabins were needed to shelter the workers tasked with blasting tunnels through the solid rock at Donner Summit.

Living in tents was easier in the desert, as the heat could be relentless. Reporters who visited the Central Pacific during construction noted that the Chinese often dug into the sand, sleeping in their "dugouts" as a way to escape the heat.

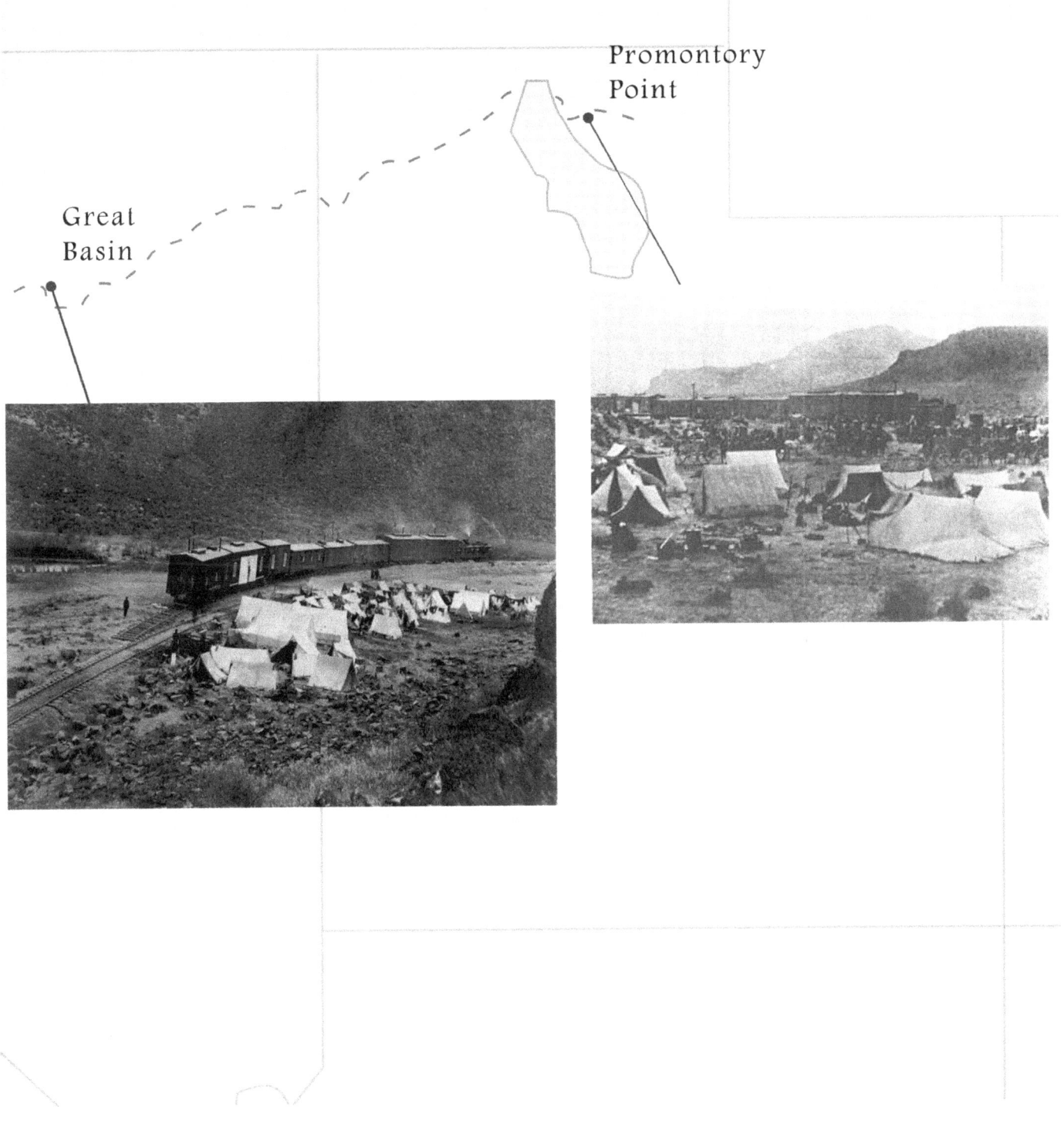

Great
Basin

Promontory
Point

In Utah, work progressed quickly, as the Union Pacific and Central Pacific each tried to be the first to reach the final destination at Promontory Point. While tent camps were used during this initial construction phase, in later years Chinese who stayed on to maintain the line sometimes made their homes in abandoned boxcars parked along the railroad, as was the case at the Carlin Maintenance Station in Nevada.

# Rock, Wood, and Metal

At Donner Summit, the campsite was occupied longer than most. The Chinese railroad workers used materials at hand to build their mountain camp and took advantage of an outcropping of granite that overlooked Donner Lake. Alfred A. Hart was the official Central Pacific photographer. He took this photograph in 1866, soon after the construction of the Summit Camp, while the workers were still building the railroad.

Some of the features at the archaeological site known as Summit Camp correspond to cabins illustrated in the Hart photograph. When archaeologists arrived to document Summit Camp, the cabin wood was long gone. The rock foundations and metal—square-cut nails, baling wire, and other fragments— were left behind. Working from this historical photograph and evidence found on the surface, archaeologists mapped the locations of cabin sites.

To document a site, archaeologists typically clear vegetation away from the area, then measure, photograph, and draw the features that they uncover, such as cooking areas used for communal cooking. Archaeologists also excavate the site (often in units known as STPs, or shovel test pits). The intent is to find artifacts below the surface that reflect the remains of everyday life: glass bottles, tin cans, ceramics, and more.

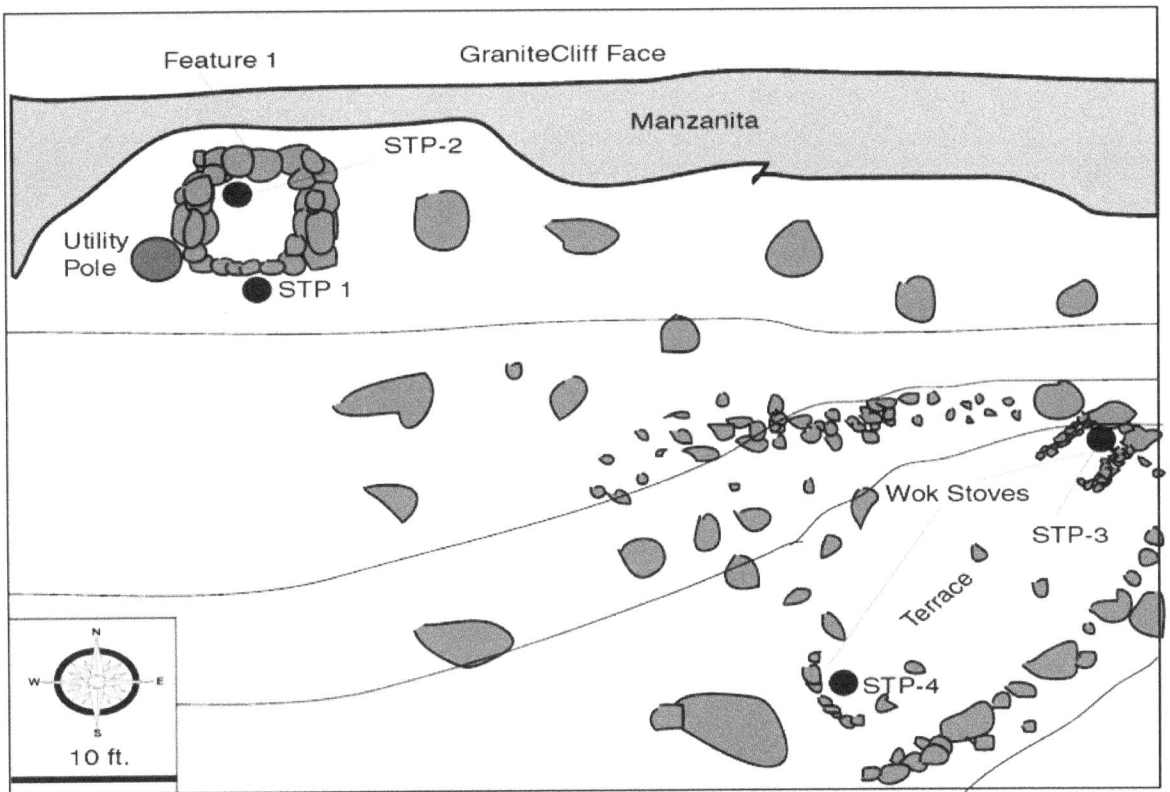

Drawings note modern intrusions, such as utility poles, as well as native stone and vegetation. Surface remnants of plastic and other modern intrusions indicated that the Summit Camp site had been disturbed; still, much information remained. Archaeologists noted this, as well as many artifact and site details, in their field notes.

# Canvas, Sticks, and Cooling Pits

### *—Chris Merritt and Mary Maniery*

Laborers must have been relieved when the work in the high Sierra was finished and they could move east, leaving behind the deep snow and cold of the mountains. Little did they know that they would face another type of environmental challenge: crossing the vast desert of the Great Basin.

In Nevada and northwestern Utah, Chinese workers faced extremely arid conditions, contended with the unique salt and mudflats of the Great Salt Lake region, and lived within the broad sweeping plains and ridges of sagebrush and juniper.

Chinese railroad workers remained dependent on the timely arrival of water and other supplies from the company, as options for procuring supplies from local communities or the surrounding environment were nonexistent. Water often had to be transported by rail or wagon 40 miles or more in order to reach the workers.

For shelters, the Chinese employed on the Central Pacific constructed earth- and/or rock-lined dugouts with canvas or sagebrush/juniper coverings, quickly adapting to the environment and leaving behind a visible archaeological signature. A Chinese worker once slept in this depression, found beside the old railroad grade in Utah, keeping cool by burrowing into the earth.

These juniper branches found along the railroad in Nevada were placed to form an A-frame and then covered with canvas to keep out the sun. The branches provided cover for a shallow depression (not visible in the photograph) dug into the sand.

A small deposit of Chinese cultural material near Monument Rock in Utah is one of the most intriguing Chinese railroad-worker sites identified to date. There archaeologists discovered a lone brown-glazed stoneware Chinese liquor jar on a small knoll overlooking the Central Pacific grade and the Great Salt Lake. These Chinese liquor-jar fragments overlay an early prehistoric component, likely from some time during the last 3,000 years. This find suggests an individual seeking a place of quiet refuge from the daily toils of railroad labor and, whether by chance or through some shared human consideration, choosing the same location at which a Native American, thousands of years earlier, may have rested and watched for game.

## Dressing the Part

Chinese workers are often illustrated wearing blue work clothes from China. Some historical photographs show more of a mix of styles. Chinese workers used many European American goods: overalls, shirts, pants, boots, and hats. Like most immigrants, the workers likely used some items that they had brought with them—like the wide-brimmed straw hats suitable for long hot days—and purchased what they needed when the work began.

Archaeological evidence only gives glimpses of the choices that Chinese workers made: scores of European-style buttons and buckles remain, along with distinctive ball-shaped Chinese buttons. Fabric and hats do not generally survive archaeologically.

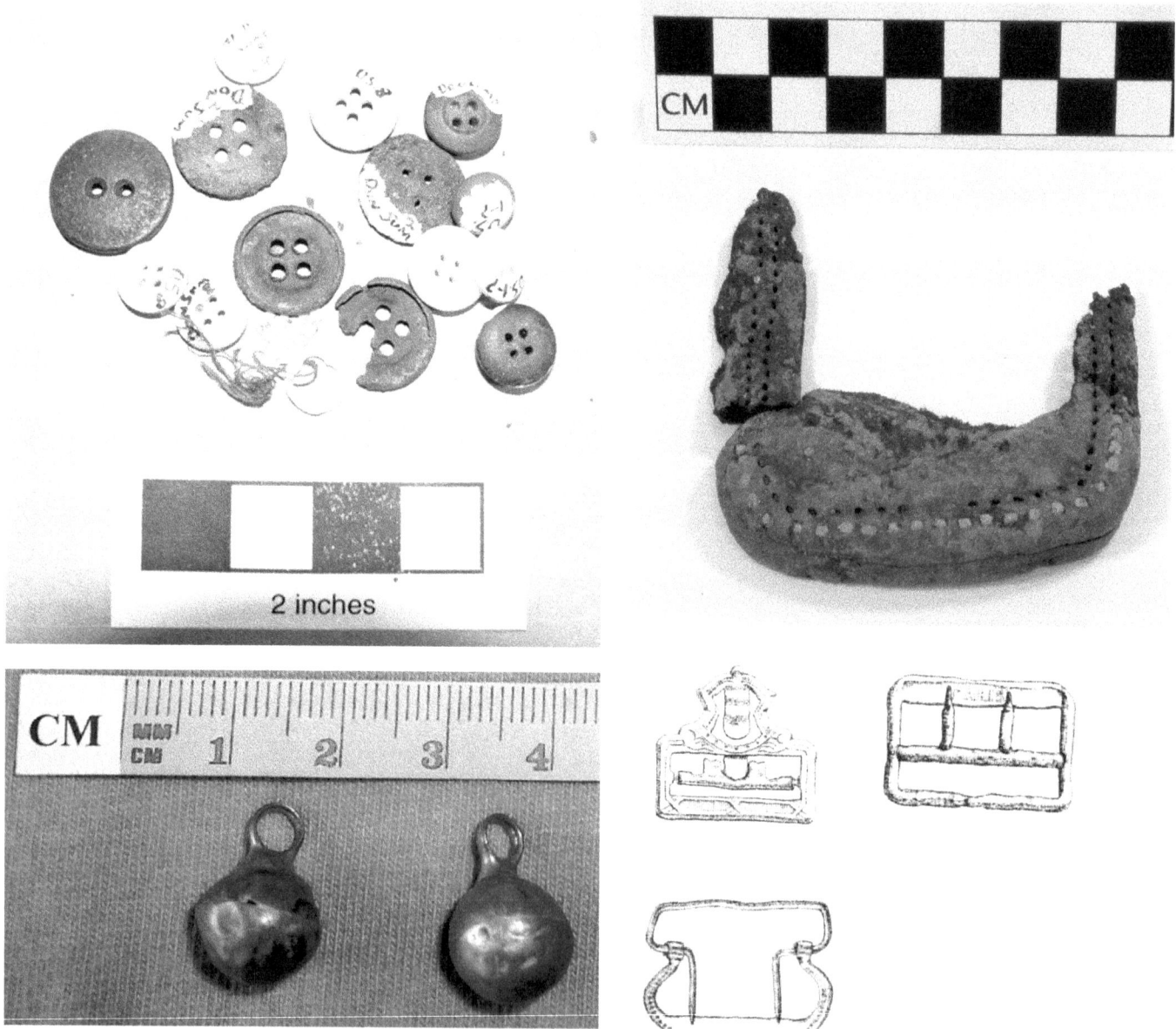

*We passed hosts of Chinamen, shortening curves and ballasting the track. Nearly four thousand are still employed in perfecting the road. They are all young, and their faces look singularly quick and intelligent. A few wear basket hats; but all have substituted boots for their wooden shoes, and adopted pantaloons and blouses.*

—*Albert D. Richardson, Letter, New York Tribune, summer of 1869*

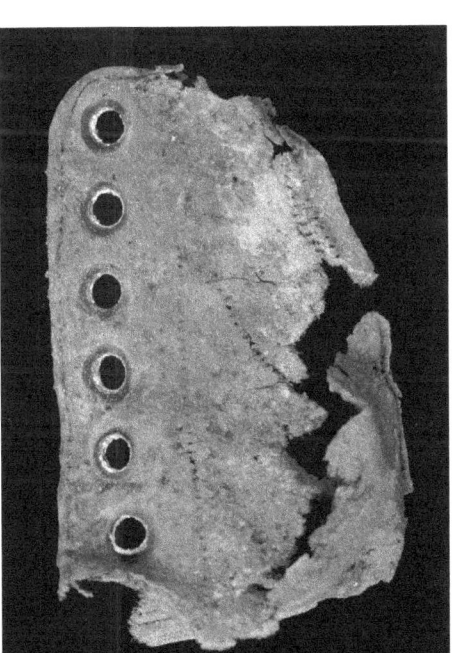

### Mining Shoes.

52380 Men's Whole Stock Kip Miners' Shoes, two buckles, dirt excluder, hob nailed, warranted, sizes. 6 to 11. Per pair $2.00 Weight, 68 ounces.

52381 Men's Whole Stock Kip Miners Shoes, lace, high cut dirt excluder, hob nailed, warranted, sizes, 6 to 11. Per pair .........$2.00 Weight, 68 ounces.

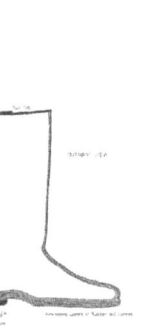

52384 Men's "A" Kip Mining Shoe, lace, medium high cut, heavy soles and broad heels to protect uppers. The bottom thoroughly hob-nailed The shoe will give excellent wear. Sizes, 6 to 11. Per pair .... $1.50 Weight, 53 ounces.

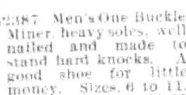

52387 Men's One Buckle Miner, heavy soles, well nailed and made to stand hard knocks. A good shoe for little money. Sizes, 6 to 11. Per pair .........$1.25 Weight, 53 ounces.

### River Shoes.

52390 Men's River or Driving Shoes, also used a great deal in the mountains, where a light shoe is of no account. Made of the very best tannery calfskin, double sole and tap put on with steel nails. The seams all riveted and cannot possibly rip, extra high cut, with four rings and strap lace, with buckle at top, making a very neat appearing shoe. Every pair warranted. Sizes, 6 to 11. Price....$3.75 Weigh, 56 oz.

52392 Men's River or Driving Shoe, made exactly the same as 52390, only the stock is real calf, making a little heavier shoes; every pair warranted. Sizes, 6 to 11. Price, per pair ....$3.25 Weight, 56 ounces.

Occasional fragments of footwear are found in the archaeological record and allow for artist reconstructions of what the workers were wearing. Contemporary newspaper advertisements and historical photographs are a complementary source for determining what was available to the Chinese workers. Clothing worn during the day may have varied from clothing worn in the evenings, when the workers relaxed.

## Stretching the Budget

Especially in a remote location, where bringing in supplies was often a challenge, and money was always scarce, workers learned to reuse what was at hand. Archaeologists find many reminders of their thriftiness: flattened cans that could be used as roofing or to patch holes in the wall; metal punched to use as sieves or strainers; cut bits of metal that served as substitutes for gaming pieces; metal scraps rolled to form funnels; and 40-gallon powder kegs reused as bathing tubs.

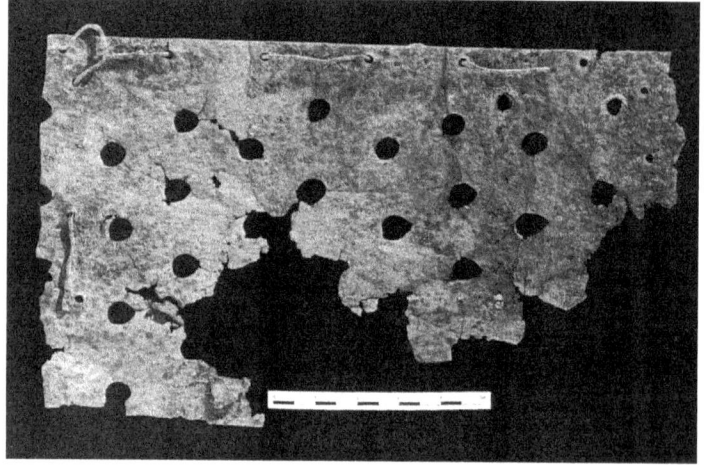

Railroad company accounts note some of the food brought to the workers: dried oysters and abalone, dried bamboo, seaweed, mushrooms, dried fruits, rice, crackers, vermicelli, salted cabbage, Chinese sugar, peanut oil, Chinese bacon, pork, and poultry. In some instances workers were known to raise chickens and pigs. Near Donner Pass, a small pond at an elevation of 7,000 feet is still stocked with catfish, a remnant of the workers' desire for fresh fish. They also likely added to their diet by hunting deer and other wild game.

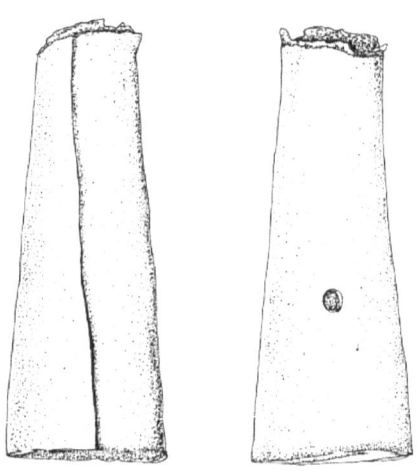

# 3
# Defining Identity

On the monument plaque:

## CHINESE RAILROAD WORKERS

ABOUT 1000 FEET FROM THIS LOCATION IS THE TRACK OF THE TRANSCONTINENTAL RAILROAD. IN 1865 THOUSANDS OF CHINESE IN KWANTUNG PROVINCE CHINA WERE RECRUITED TO WORK ON THIS GREAT CONNECTION BETWEEN THE EAST AND WEST COAST. THIS MONUMENT IS DEDICATED TO THE MEMORY OF THOSE CHINESE LABORERS WHO WORKED FOR CHARLES CROCKER OF THE CENTRAL PACIFIC RAILROAD.

TABLET PLACED WITH THE COOPERATION BETWEEN THE STATE DEPARTMENT OF TRANSPORTATION AND THE PLACER COUNTY HISTORICAL SOCIETY
JULY 3, 2009

Building the Railroad

Adapting to a New Environment

Defining Identity

Health and Well-Being

Leisure

Leaving a Legacy

Appendices

# Finding the Past

Archaeologists are trained to interpret abandoned remnants of past lives and to identify who worked, played, lived out their lives on the land, what they were doing to support themselves, and when they were there. Archaeologists also strive to learn about the cultural heritage of the person, family, or group—where they came from—all based on the discarded artifacts and features left behind.

Some sites cannot be missed. The broken bottles, fragmented dishes, cans, and metal are visible on the landscape; house outlines are marked with rock walls or cleared areas; and evidence of human activity is all around. Other sites need a trained eye to interpret the subtle changes in the landscape that can mark a work area or other previous occupation.

The most important task of the archaeologist is to examine the features and artifacts and combine that information with the historical record and oral histories to interpret when and how a site was used, and who may have lived there. All late 19th-century railroad-worker camps (regardless of which group lived there) contain similar artifacts, such as glass bottles once filled with medicine, condiments, or alcohol, as well as ceramic storage jars and dishes made in the United States or England, tin cans, and sheet metal. Camps occupied by Chinese workers also contain distinct kinds of artifacts, many made in China, that are rare or lacking in the camps occupied by non-Chinese.

# Pecked Marks on a Bowl

Perhaps one of the most frustrating aspects of research for archaeologists and historians studying Chinese railroad workers is the lack of documents written by the railroad workers themselves. Payroll ledgers with English versions of Chinese names still exist. Although railroad workers may have sent letters home and to each other, none of these has survived in archives within the United States.

Archaeologists discovered that some of the bowl fragments at Summit Camp had peck marks. Similar marks had been seen on bowls found in railroad towns, such as Folsom, Truckee, and Carlin. Researchers guessed that the peck markings indicate individual or company ownership of bowls, or symbols of good luck. As most meals were communal, marking a bowl suggests individuality: "I was here" or "It is mine."

This mark from a ceramic bowl found at Summit Camp transliterates as *xing*, meaning apricot or almond. It could also be a surname, indicating ownership.

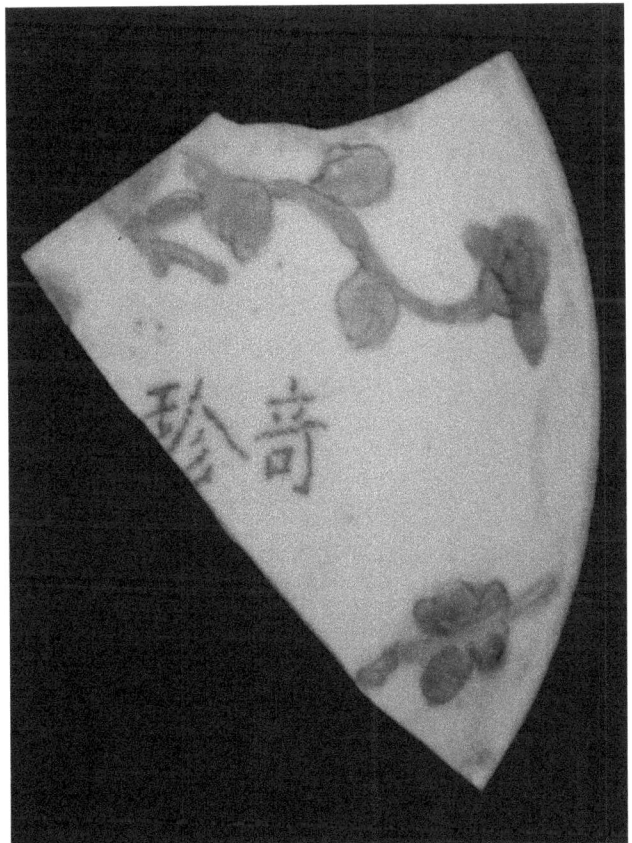

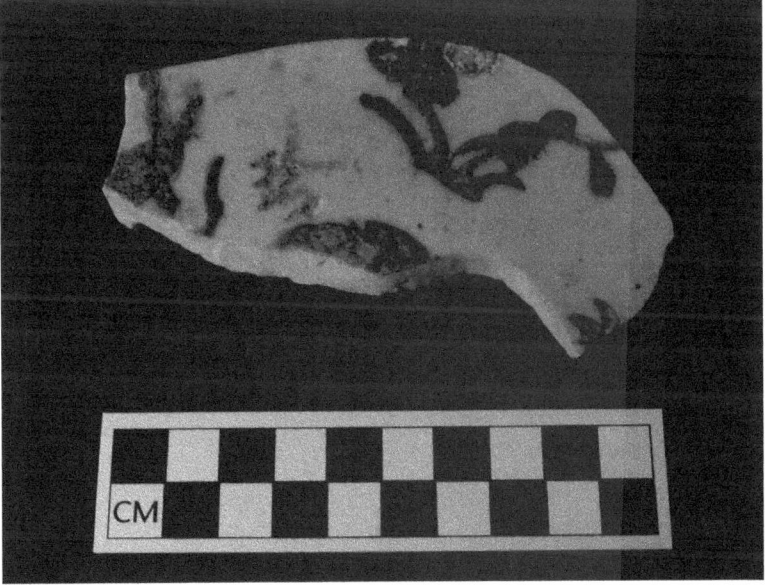

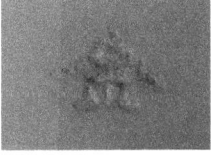

Plates recovered from the Folsom Chinatown, adjacent to the Central Pacific yard, are pecked with a mark meaning "rare treasure" that could represent a business or restaurant name. "Treasure" or "Zhen" (a woman's first name), and "gold/Jin" (probably an ownership mark).

## Cooking the Chinese Way

Chinese cooking methods are distinct from those of American or European kitchens, both in the past and today. While cooks were quick to incorporate locally available foods into their diet, archaeological evidence suggests that they cooked food in ways familiar to them. Pots and pans, food preparation and cooking utensils, and even the marks left on discarded bones provide clues for archaeologists to use when establishing the identities of a site's past occupants.

Long-handled spatulas were handy when stir-frying in woks. While the bamboo or wood handles are rarely found on archaeological sites, the metal is remarkably durable. The rounded shape of the spatula head, wide surface, and long handle are distinctive characteristics of a utensil designed for Chinese cooking.

Archaeologists have found fragments of cast-iron wok pieces and handles at Summit Camp and in the Chinatowns along the railroad, like the Folsom examples shown here. These flat, thick, and heavy pieces indicate to the archaeologist that Chinese cooking took place there.

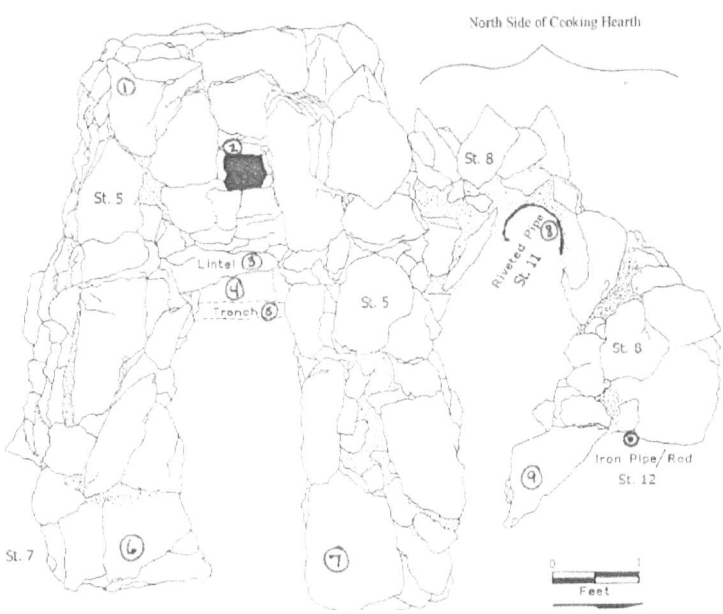

A typical feature at Chinese camps is a low, hairpin or U-shaped hearth. Archaeologists pay special attention to these features and carefully photograph and draw them to scale.

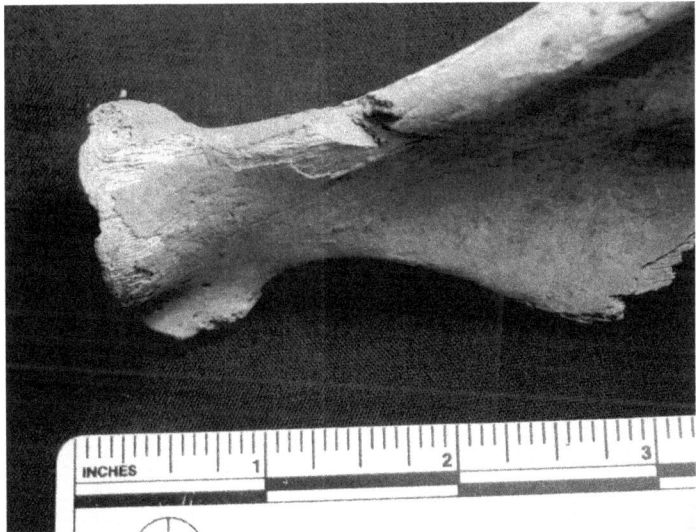

Cleavers manufactured in China were the preferred all-purpose implement used in Chinese kitchens, both then and now. The cleaver would have had a wooden handle. Archaeologically, these uniquely shaped cleavers are one clue that Chinese cooks were present on a site. Within many railroad camp sites, archaeologists find evidence of animal bones cut with saws, a European American technique. Chinese may have procured meat from local butchers, but then used cleavers to further process the meat in the camps. The cuts that cleavers leave on animal bones during chopping and butchering are archaeologically distinctive.

## Comfort Food

Preparing and consuming foods familiar from home must have brought some comfort to railroad workers. At most camps occupied by Chinese workers, archaeologists find fragments of tin cans (once holding preserved foods) and storage jars made in the United States, as well as brown-glazed stoneware jars and vessels made in the Guangdong Province. These utilitarian jars were packed with pickled, dried, and preserved foods. Newspaper ads from Truckee and other towns along the railroad often mention the availability of "Chinese Merchandice" in the local stores, suggesting that food products from China were readily available to the workers along the Central Pacific route.

Barrel jars came in a variety of sizes and were used to ship food products overseas. Store ledgers suggest they were packed with preserved vegetables, preserved duck eggs, and other southern China foodstuffs. Photographs and accounts from newspapers indicate that they were often reused to hold tea, gunpowder, rice, and beans.

Globular stoneware jars most likely contained vinegar, liquor, or soy sauce. Ceramic "bows" found on the jars' shoulders have hollow centers, allowing the lid to be secured in place with twine or rope.

Small, squat jars like this are another type of stoneware food-storage vessel commonly found at Chinese camps. These held dried vegetables or fermented soybean sauces, such as *nom yue* or *fu yue*.

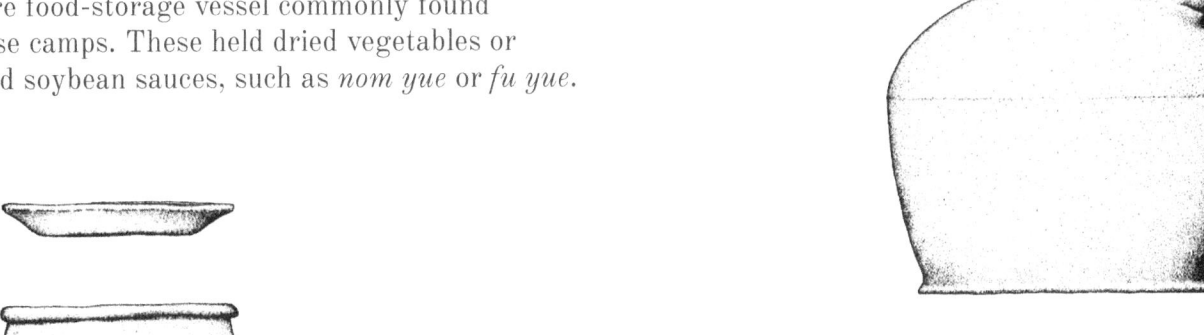

The rolled ring lips and spouts from these small jars are frequently identified on campsites. Archaeologists often find these sturdy vessels unbroken, a remarkable thing, considering they were last used 150 years ago! These jars were shipped from Canton in Guangdong Province, a region known as a major producer of soy sauce. Besides the soy sauce, they were used to ship liquor, vinegar, and other liquids.

# A Bowl for Every Man

Ceramic fragments of plain white bowls, saucers, and plates made in the United States or China are found at most railroad camps. One clue used to distinguish Chinese-occupied camps is the addition of blue-and-white ceramic bowls made in China found on the site. *Min yao* is a term for folk ware: these inexpensive bowls were made with two distinct patterns—Double Happiness and Bamboo—and were everyday wares used in the houses of common folk in China and brought over to the United States. These familiar bowls may have been one small way the men laboring in the camps connected with the traditional and everyday home life they had left behind.

Double Happiness is the name given to this pattern in a 19th-century Chinese store ledger found in California. The pattern consists of swirls and the Double Happiness symbol hand painted in blue on a white background. This pattern is most frequently found throughout the West on sites occupied before 1870. Archaeologists recovered pieces of bowls with this pattern at Summit Camp, China Kitchen, and other sites along the railroad in the high Sierra.

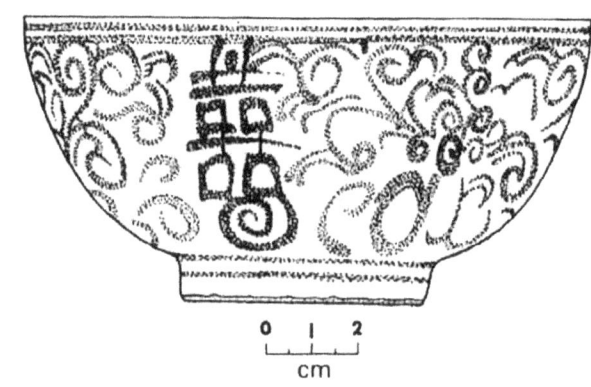

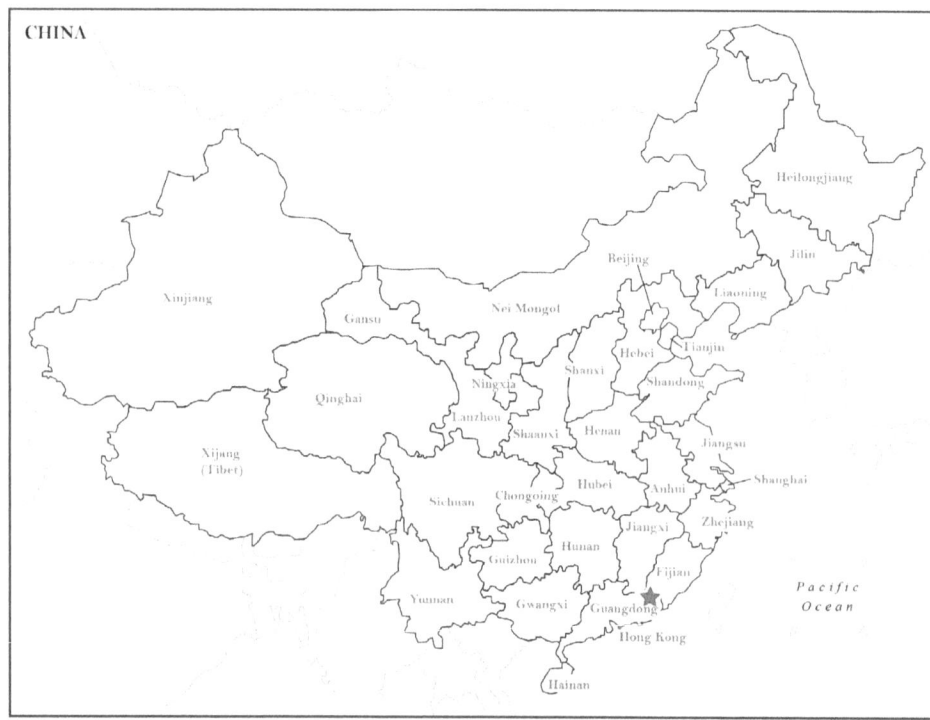

*Both Bamboo and Double Happiness rice bowls were manufactured in the eastern region of Guangdong, in Dabu County in the Mei Xian Prefecture. In the surrounding hillsides are numerous kilns. 40 kilometers (24.8 miles) to the south of Dabu City is the town of Gao Bi (Gaopizhen). Surrounding Gao Bi are kilns in Zhou Rui, Ping Yuan, Guang De, Tao Yuen, and Tan Jiang. These kilns produce folk ceramics (min yao) for the common people.*

*—Philip Choy, historian, 2014*

*In Chinese, all blue-and-white porcelain and porcelaneous stonewares are generically described as* ching hua. *The character* ching *denotes the blue and blue-green color of the wares. The character* hua *means "flower," but it is also used to denote other design patterns.*

**—Philip Choy, historian, 2014**

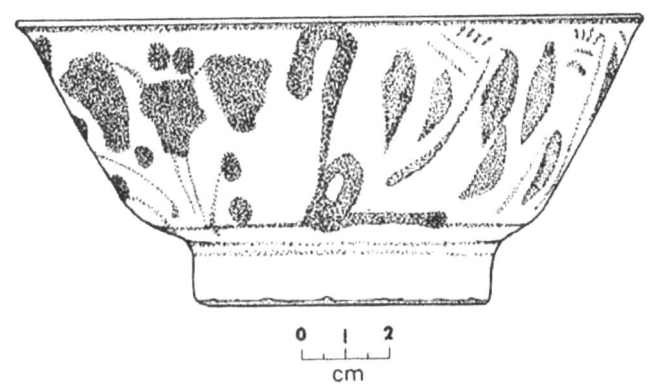

The pattern referred to as "Bamboo," also using a name assigned in a 19th-century store ledger, represents a field of bamboo and blossoms, and a rock. Produced primarily near the seaport of Swatow (Shantou), Bamboo is the most common bowl pattern found on western sites occupied by Chinese after about 1868. It has been found at Chinese camps along the railroad, particularly in Nevada and Utah, and at camps associated with later railroad building efforts, such as the Virginia-Truckee in Nevada, Northern Pacific in Montana and Idaho, and Southern Pacific routes as far east as Langley, Texas.

# Serving Soups and Sauces

While found in lesser numbers than Bamboo or Double Happiness, two other patterns, Winter Green and Four Season Flower, have been identified in the camps, especially at those used for longer periods of time, like Summit Camp and Carlin.

*Jingdezhen in northeast Jiangxi Province is renowned as the porcelain capital of China, producing ceramics for the Imperial Court. However, the profusion of kilns in the region also manufactured folk wares of cups, plates, bowls, spoons and other forms for use by common people. The Winter Green and Four Season Flower ceramics are from these Jingdezhen kilns.*

—**Philip Choy, historian, 2014**

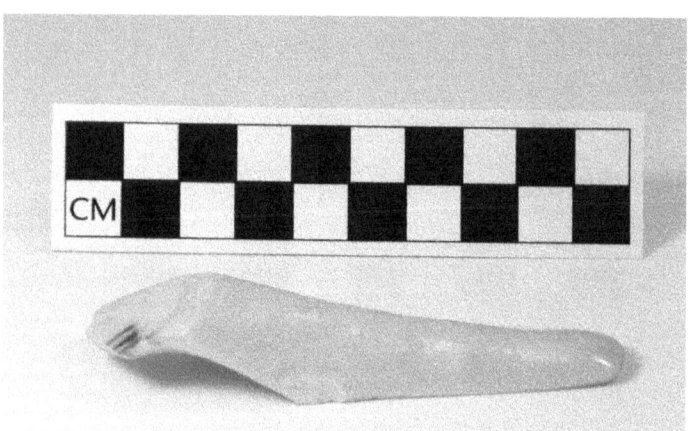

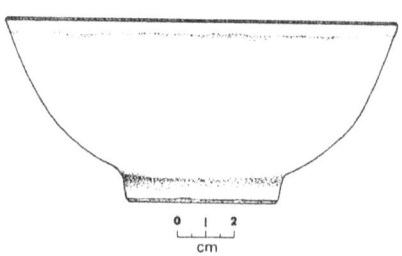

The Winter Green pattern is found on bowls, spoons, and cups and is defined by a greenish exterior glaze and a clear or white interior. Blue marks are usually found on the base. Often referred to as "celadon," the fragments of ceramic vessels with this bright green glaze are easy for archaeologists to spot on a site and indicate a Chinese-immigrant occupation.

The Four Season Flower pattern consists of clearly identifiable floral elements representing the four seasons: spring (peony), summer (lotus), fall (chrysanthemum), and winter (plum). This pattern dates back to the Chia Ching reign (1796–1821) during the Ching dynasty.

Unlike the Bamboo and Double Happiness patterns that appear only on bowls, Winter Green and Four Season Flower patterns decorated different sizes of bowls, plates, spoons, and cups. The widest variety of forms occurs in the Four Season Flower pattern and includes spoons, large serving bowls and plates, medium and small sauce plates, and tiny, small, and medium cups. While most commonly found in the towns or cities that serviced the railroad (Truckee, Auburn, Folsom, Carlin), some of these vessels made their way to the camps for archaeologists to find.

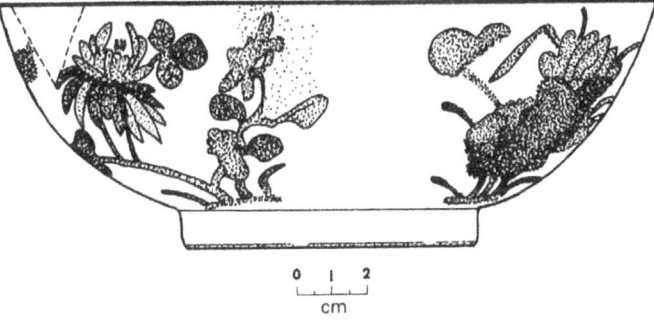

# A Popular Import

Fueled by European American social mores and fears of addiction, there are many misconceptions and stereotypes regarding opium use among the Chinese. In reality, taking small doses of opium was similar to taking modern pain relievers after a day of hard work. Many patent medicines manufactured in the United States in the late 19th century also contained opiates. Given the intense physical effort expended every single day by workers, it is perhaps not surprising that evidence of opiate use (whether bottled in glass in the United States or imported from China) is a common find on railroad sites.

Brass opium tins imported from China are easily identified at archaeological sites. First, brass does not rust; the silver or burnished color of the metal stands out on sites full of rusty cans and metal scrap. Second, they have impressed characters or cartouches in the lid. In rare cases, they retain paper labels, customs stamps, or other identifying marks.

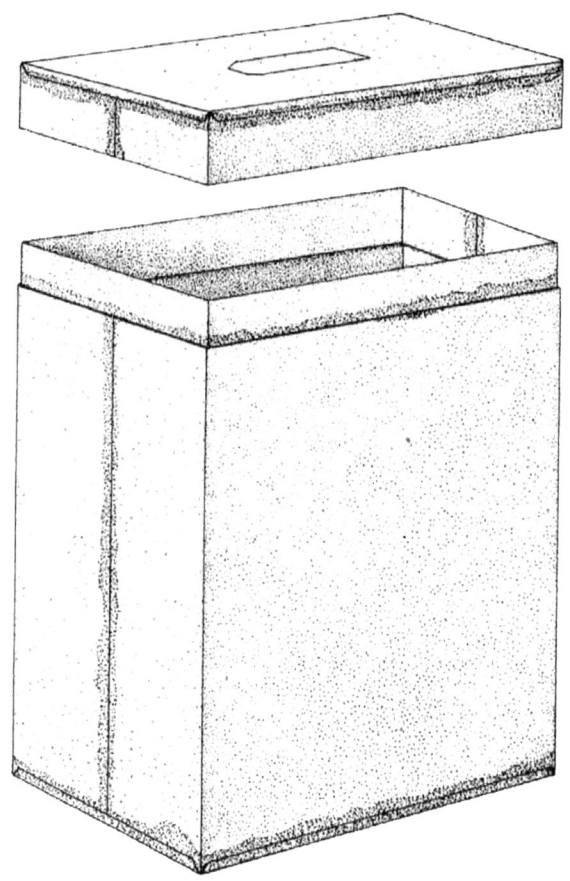

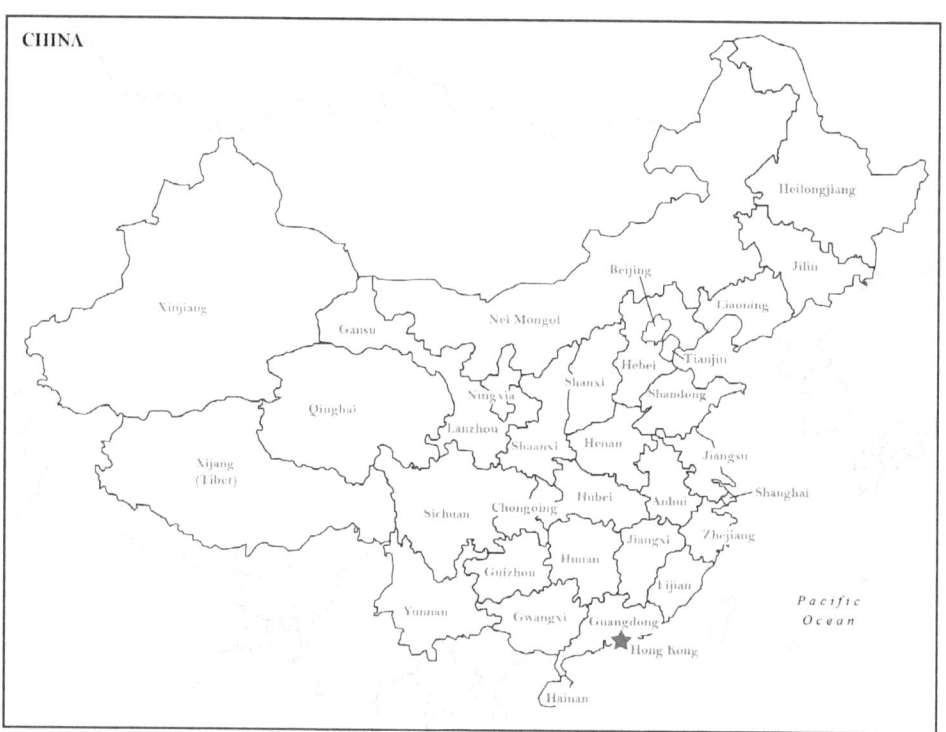

Sometimes, soil conditions, climate, and artifact locations create unique circumstances that result in preservation of fragile materials. Remnants of bright orange paper labels have been found on some of the brass opium tins recovered in Folsom and a few other railroad towns and camps. Translations of these labels indicate that the product was sold and imported from the Shanghuan District in Hong Kong.

While most of the labels give guarantees regarding the quality of the product, a few provide dates. This label (ca. 1859), for example, translates as:

> Since the day of opening, we do not have any branches or different stores. Recently there are some smugglers selling fake goods. Our store does not like to deceive customers. Everybody is welcome to our store. Please recognize our trademark. Written by Huo You Xin in the ninth year of Xian Feng.

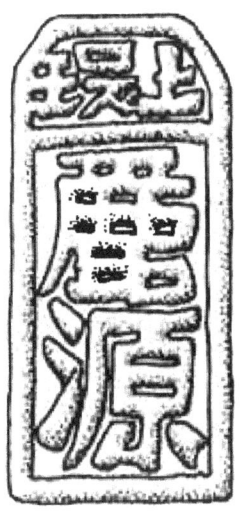

The cartouches containing characters stamped into the lids of opium tins are believed to represent the brand name or quality of the opium. This cartouche, recovered from a camp in Bovine, Utah, is one of the most common recovered at archaeological sites and represents Li Yun or "beautiful origin" brand opium. Opium tins with this cartouche have been found in railroad camps throughout the West.

# More Evidence of the Familiar

Chinese and Vietnamese coins were used as money, worn on cords around necks for good luck, or used in place of glass markers in gaming. These multipurpose currencies have been recovered at many Chinese sites along the railroad.

Small glass pieces were made in China and used as gaming markers. They were small enough to fit in a pocket and easily misplaced. They have made their way onto a few of the work camps, including Summit Camp.

Archaeologists have identified fragments of traditional stoneware Chinese oil lamps at campsites in the high Sierra and in railroad towns like Carlin. In this example, a wick was placed in peanut or animal oil and lit, providing a portable light that would have been essential for living along the railroad.

Chinese medicine bottles were small enough to move with personal belongings from campsite to campsite. While patent medicines made in the United States are found at all railroad work camps, the small green or aqua Chinese-made vials are often found on the sites used by Chinese workers.

Bulbous stoneware bottles with flared lips contained Chinese liquor or wine. While whole bottles are not often recovered on sites, the flared lips are a durable and lasting reminder of the role Chinese played in building the Central Pacific Railroad.

# 4
# Health and Well-Being

## Hazards of the Job

Railroad work was dangerous and labor intensive. To get paid, workers had to remain able-bodied. In spite of their efforts to maintain good health and protect their well-being, many Chinese died or were seriously injured as a result of explosions, cave-ins, avalanches, and severe and unpredictable weather. Many Chinese railroad workers also perished from disease.

*A violent sand storm passed over the country in the vicinity of Humboldt Lake, on the afternoon of the Sunday last. For a time the wind blew so violently and the sand and dirt was so thick in the air that it was impossible to see ten paces. The Chinese tents in the vicinity of Brown's station, on the railroad, were generally leveled to the ground, and much of their light house goods scattered by the winds.*

—*Daily Alta California, August 12, 1868*

Newspaper articles frequently reported on railroad workers' deaths from disease, accidents and explosions, and natural disasters.

**BONES OF DEFUNCT CHINAMEN.—**The Central Pacific freight train last evening brought to the city the bones of about fifty defunct Chinamen, who died from disease or were killed by accident while working on the line of the Central Pacific Railroad. They are to be interred in Conboie's private cemetery, as have been already the bones of about one hundred others similarly deceased.

*There are at present a number of cases of small-pox along the "front" of the line of the Central Pacific Railroad, and on Thursday last night there was a death from the disease at Argenta.*

*—Territorial Enterprise, January 5, 1869*

**KILLED BY AN AVALANCHE.—**The Dutch Flat *Enquirer*, December 25th, is informed by a man from the Summit that on Saturday a gang of Chinamen employed on the Railroad were covered up by a snow slide and some four or five of them died before they could be exhumed. Snow storms accompanied with high winds made the stay at the Summit anything but agreeable, the snow being from ten to fifteen feet deep; notwithstanding which the road is kept open and the sleighs of the Pioneer Company make their regular trips to Cisco. The snow fell to such a depth on Friday that one whole camp of Chinamen was covered up during the night, and parties were digging them out when our informant left.

*My father came over. My uncle came over. Unfortunately my uncle lost an eye blasting across the snow shed.*

*—Kim Hong, railroad-worker descendant, 1994*

For more serious ailments, such as smallpox, the railroad hired Chinese doctors, like Fong Dun Shing. Many Chinese laborers did not trust Western doctors or Western medicine. Around 1870, Fong Dun Shing stopped working for the railroad and opened an herbal shop, Kwong Tsui Chang (success peacefully), on I Street in Sacramento.

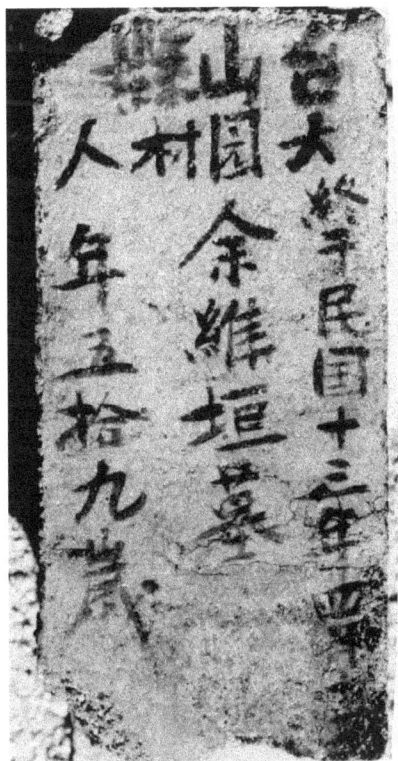

This is an "identity brick" buried with Yee Wai-yuan, who may have done maintenance work for the Central Pacific in the former railroad town of Carlin, Nevada.

*Archaeological studies of Chinese skeletal remains give clues to their experience in the American west. Robust skeletons and degenerative joint changes attest to the strenuous labor these men performed.*

*—Sue Fawn Chung, historian, and John Joseph Crandall, bioarchaeologist, 2014*

## Ancient and Effective

Chinese medicine has been practiced for over 2,000 years and is empirical, that is, based on observation and experimentation; and holistic, focused on treating the body as an integrated whole rather than as a series of isolated parts. Medical knowledge was (and still is) valued in Chinese culture, and railroad workers likely had a basic understanding of the causes of and treatments for disease.

Chinese merchants established stores in towns near the railroad route, and sold herbal medicines to workers. Workers may have also visited Chinese doctors practicing in these towns.

**DR. OFFO,**
**CHINESE PHYSICIAN**—OFFICE, FRONT street, between I and J streets, up stairs, Sacramento, offers his services to the public for the successful treatment of Consumption, Bronchitis, Kidney Affections, Dyspepsia, Affections of the Lungs, Fevers, Diarrhea, Sore Eyes, Felum, Fever Sores, Private Diseases, and all Diseases of the human frame.
Terms, reasonable. Remember the place:
DR. OFFO,
Front street between I and J sts., up stairs.

Herbal remedies were popular for medical treatment and could be taken internally or applied externally as a powder or paste. Although "herbal" implies a plant-based remedy, Chinese herbal medicines contained mixtures of plants, animal parts like this dried gecko below, and minerals.

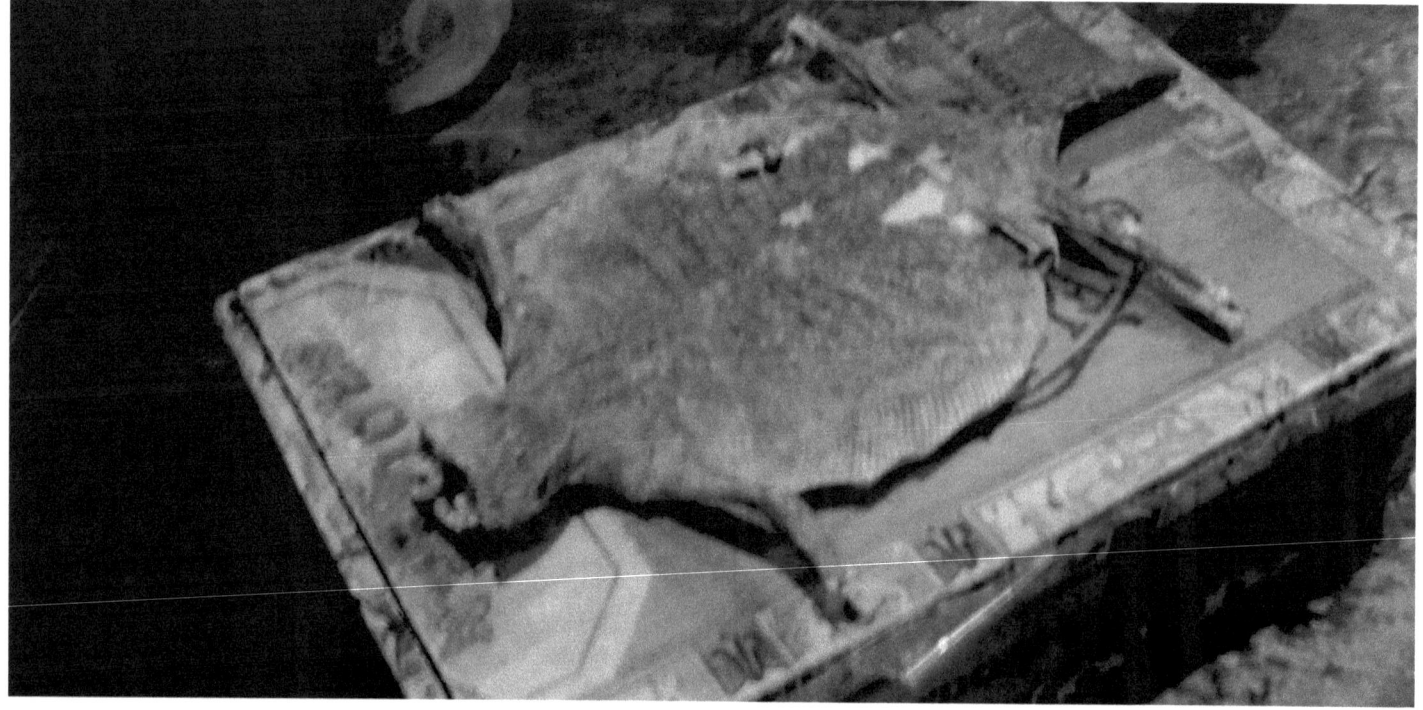

# Easing Aches and Pains

Liquid opium was sold as a medicinal drug in the 19th century, popular predominantly among European Americans, who used it to treat a variety of conditions, including headaches, neurological disorders, throat and lung ailments, teething pain in children, and venereal diseases.

Among Chinese workers, opium was used to help relieve aches and pains from long hours of backbreaking work, such as grading and laying track for the railroads. Rather than a liquid, opium was typically exported from China in solid form, but could also come in small pellets or pills.

Railroad workers also used a variety of external treatments to relax sore muscles and joints, and to treat skin injuries, such as burns. External treatments consisted of the application of herbal ingredients to the surface of the skin in the form of plasters and poultices, and the use of various objects or tools to stimulate different muscle groups and nerve endings.

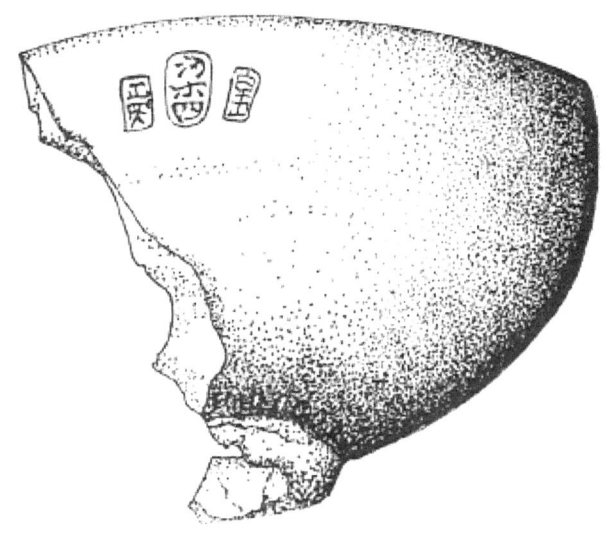

Opium lamps, spoons, brass saddles, and pipe-bowl fragments, such as this one, are often recovered from Chinese railroad camps.

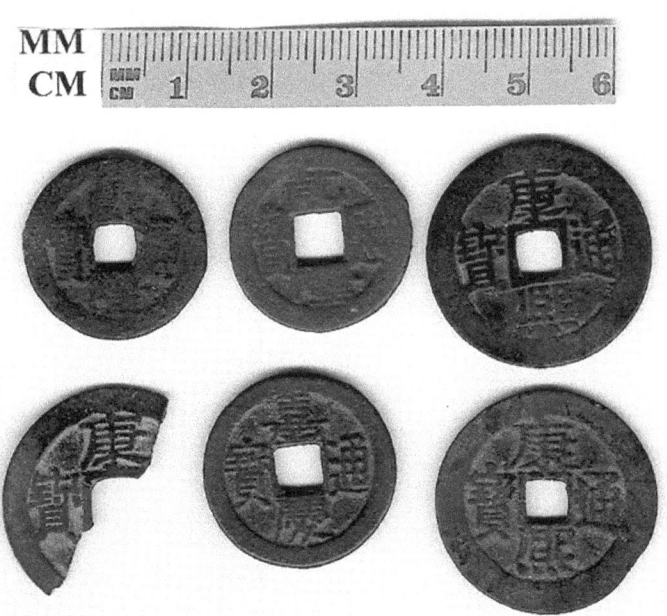

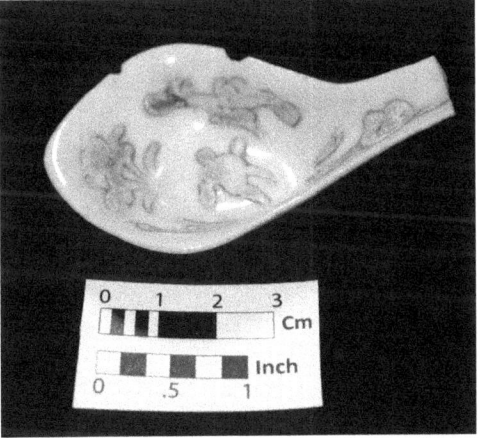

Brass and zinc coins of various denominations and soup spoons have been found at most Chinese railroad camps. Besides their more utilitarian functions, these objects could have been used to perform *guā shā*, or scraping. This technique involves application of regular pressure, in a stroke-like movement, to areas of the body where pain, heat, and improper blood flow or blood stagnation occur

# Healthy Habits

Maintaining one's health through a balanced diet and good hygiene was a way that Chinese workers took care of themselves in remote railroad camps. Boiling water for tea sterilized water taken from streams and lakes. As a result, Chinese railroad workers had lower rates of dysentery than European American railroad workers.

The queue, or long braid, was a male hairstyle required by law in Qing dynasty China. During work, men often coiled the queue on top of their heads or tucked it under a hat. On rest days, workers often helped one another re-braid the long queue. This custom of wearing the queue ended in 1911 when the Qing dynasty was overthrown, and China became a republic.

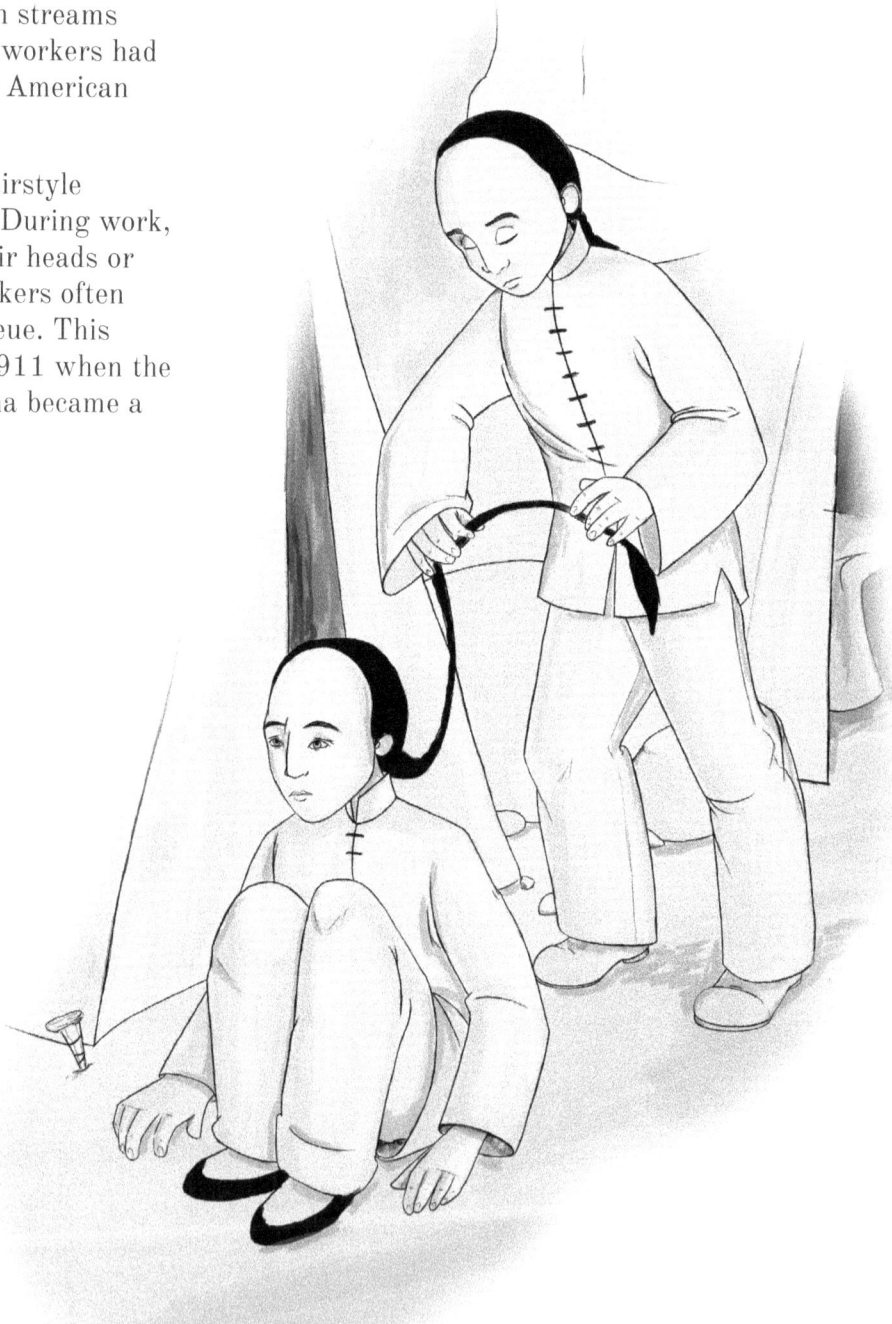

*The Chinese on the Central Pacific were divided into small groups. Each group had a cook who not only prepared their meals, but also kept a large boiler of hot water ready every night so that when the Chinese came off the road they could fill their tubs made from powder kegs and take a hot sponge bath.*

—Erle Heath, From Trail to Rail, 1927

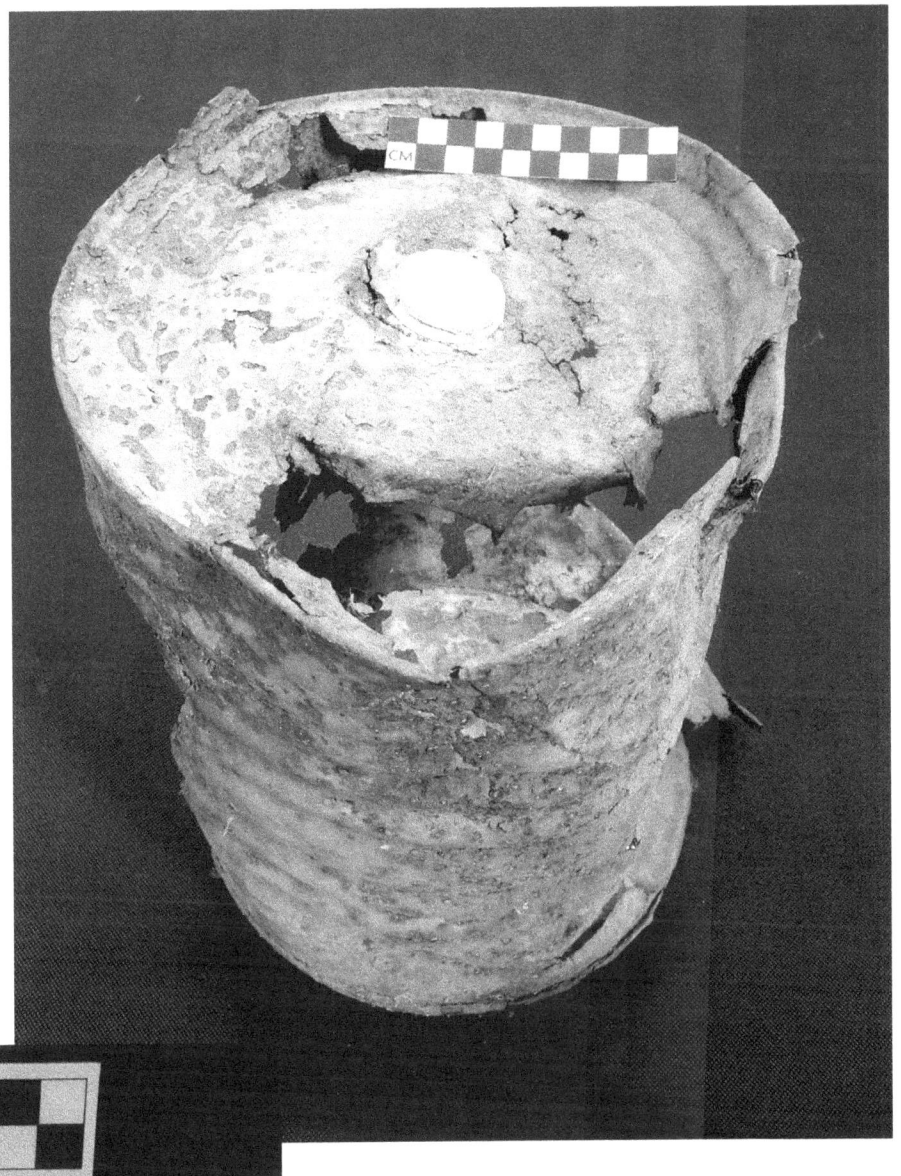

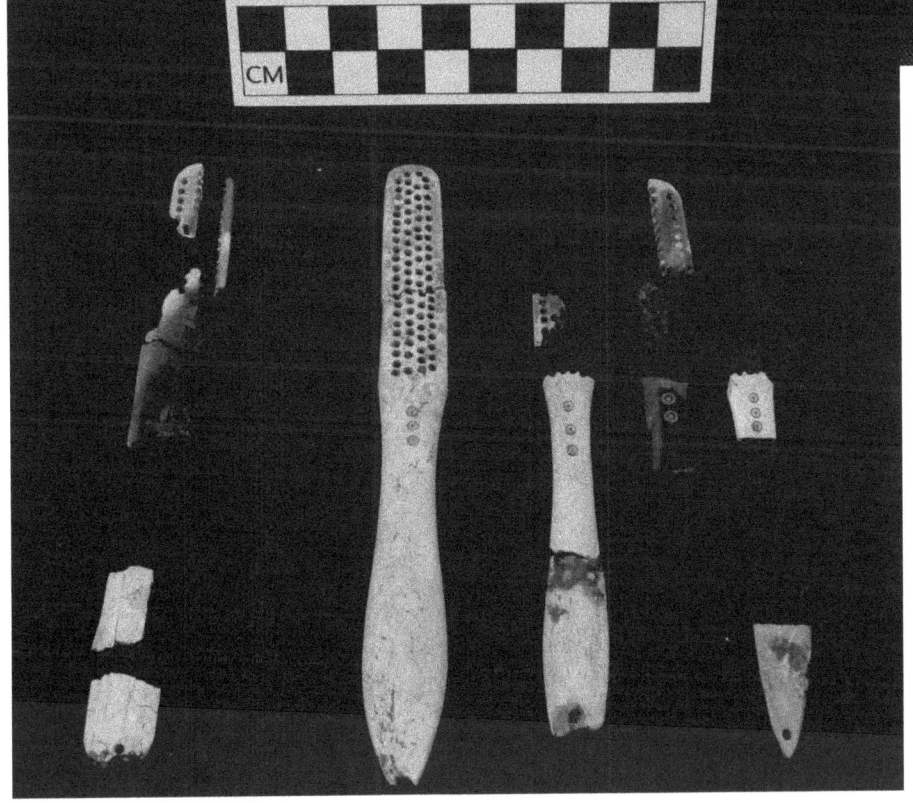

Good oral hygiene is essential in helping to ward off cavities and gum disease. The Chinese are credited with inventing the first toothbrush in the 1490s. Chinese examples, made of bone, had four or five rows of holes drilled into the head of the toothbrush and had scoring on the back. Boar hair was threaded through the holes and glued in place.

## Soup and Tea

Consuming soup was a popular method of taking herbal medicine internally. To prepare a medicinal soup, herbal ingredients were cooked in an earthenware pot with water until most of the liquid had evaporated. The decocted herbs were then mixed with other ingredients (meat/vegetables) in a soup.

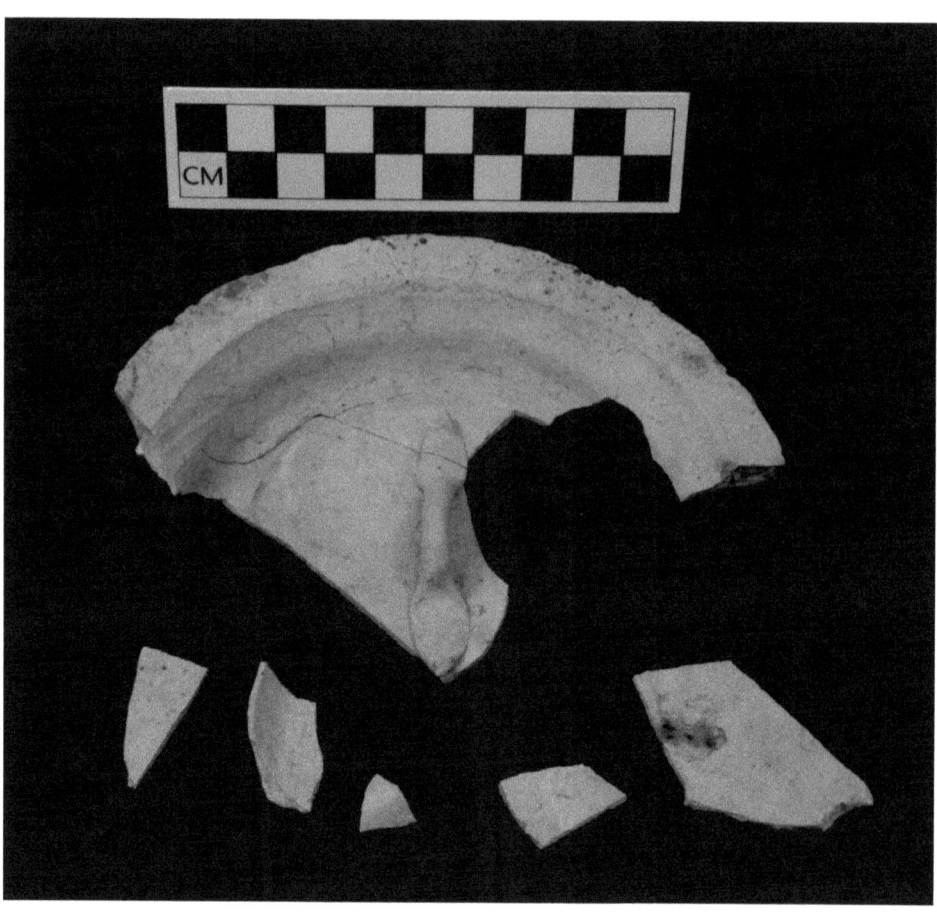

Herbal teas were prepared by either infusing or decocting herbs. To prepare an infusion of herbal tea, the herbs were placed in a ceramic pot and boiling water was poured over them. The herbs were then allowed to steep for 15–20 minutes. To make a decoction of herbal tea, herbs were strained after they had been allowed to simmer.

Teapot fragments are often found on archaeological sites. This teapot features a simple blue-and-white painting of two men engaged in a conversation.

This stoneware jug was found in a Chinese camp next to the original Central Pacific grade near Beowawe, Nevada. It likely held water or tea. Note the pig-shaped feet on this jug.

*The Chinese drank luke-warm tea. It stood beside the grade in thirty and forty-gallon whiskey barrels, always on tap. Several times daily a Chinese mess attendant brought fresh tea, pouring it into the big barrel. These beverage reinforcements were carried to the work site in powder kegs suspended from each end of a bamboo pole which was balanced on a ... shoulder.*

—*Erle Heath, From Trail to Rail, 1927*

# Internal Medicine

Small Chinese medicine bottles or vials are common finds on railroad camps. These vials typically contained a single dose of a pill, powder, or medicinal oil. These inexpensive medicines were a popular form of self-treatment among the Chinese.

This Chinese medicine bottle (shown at right) was found at a railroad maintenance and repair headquarters in Terrace, Utah. It is unusual in that it still retains its paper label. The label roughly translates to "Our store is now open for business. Peppermint oil that we exclusively sell. Located on Ironworkers Street." Peppermint oil was taken orally to treat digestive disorders, upper-respiratory infections, and gallbladder disease. It could also be applied externally to treat muscle pain and headaches.

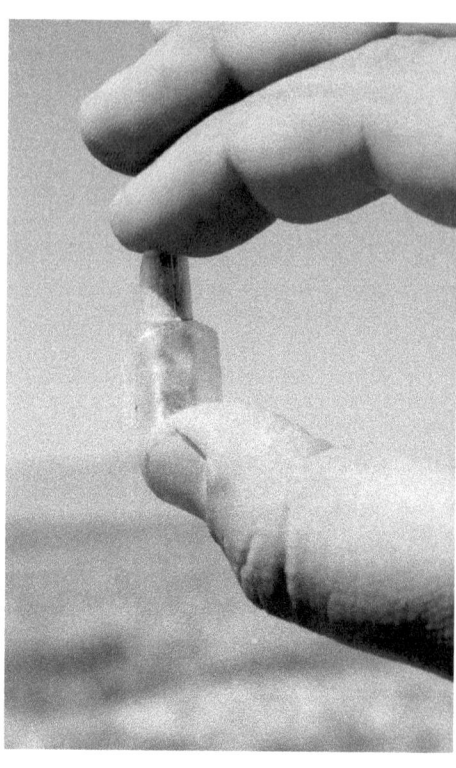

Tonic wines contained herbal ingredients distilled in liquor and were considered to have restorative powers. They could increase one's energy flow, or qi, enhance blood circulation, strengthen the kidneys, and treat rheumatism. *Mei gui lu jiu*, or rose-essence wine, was a tonic/medicinal wine that contained rosebuds and crystal sugar, and was about 50% alcohol by volume. Chinese rosebuds (*mei gui hua*) were used to treat stomach pain, indigestion, poor appetite, depression, irritability, and other ailments.

Chinese brown-glazed stoneware bottles with flared lips held rice wine or tonic wine. Fragments of these bottles are ubiquitous on Chinese archaeological sites in the West.

*The difference in the eating and drinking habits of the Chinese and white workers building the Central Pacific was as great as their other living habits. The Chinese menu included dried oysters, abalone, cuttlefish, bamboo sprouts, mushrooms, five kinds of vegetables, pork, poultry, vermicelli, rice, salted cabbage, dried seaweed, sweet rice crackers, sugar, four kinds of dried fruit, Chinese bacon, peanut oil, and tea. … The fare of the Caucasian laborer consisted of beef, beans, bread, butter, and potatoes.*

*—Erle Heath, From Trail to Rail, 1927*

Food and medicine are closely related in Chinese culture. Various food items have particular medicinal properties or "effects" associated with them. Foods have different flavors (sour, bitter, sweet, pungent, and salty), thermal properties (warming, cooling), or could be associated with various organ networks (such as the stomach or kidneys), or direction of movement (upwards, downwards, floating, or falling).

Cuttlefish (fragments from an archaeological site shown here) were a food item shipped to the U.S. in barrel jars and have been archaeologically recovered from hearths and other cooking features in rural camps. In Chinese medicine, cuttlefish bones were powdered and used primarily to stop bleeding from wounds and treating ulcers.

# Expanding the Traditional Medicine Kit

Archaeological evidence indicates that Chinese railroad workers supplemented familiar remedies imported from China with patent medicines mass-produced in the United States. Patent medicines typically contained a mixture of bitter-tasting herbs, water, alcohol, and opiates, such as morphine and nicotine.

This druggist's token, produced by J. L. Polhemus, was found at the Donner Summit Chinese camp. Druggists and other merchants, like Polhemus, who operated a drugstore in Sacramento from the 1850s to the 1870s, used tokens to advertise their businesses. It is possible that one of the railroad workers at Donner Summit visited Polhemus's drugstore.

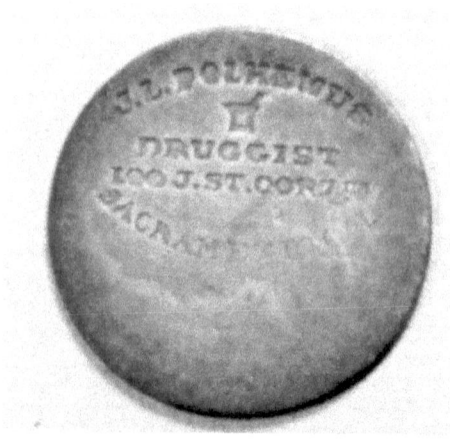

# TO DRUGGISTS.

**FOR SALE—**

 500 ounces Sulph. Quinine;
 300 lbs. Iodide Potash, A. & B.;
 500 galls Bay Rum;
 6000 lbs Flaxseed;
 3000 lbs Gum Arabic;
 5000 lbs Tartaric Acid;
 6000 lbs Alum;
 1000 lbs Camphor;
 200 lbs Oil Lemon;
 150 lbs Oil Bergamot;
 1000 lbs Borax;
 300 doz Capsules, assorted;
 100 doz Thorn's Extract;
 250 lbs Chloroform;
 250 lbs Calomel;
 10,000 lbs Chloride Lime;
 400 lbs Spirits Nitre;
 500 lbs Aqua Ammonia;
 300 galls Castor Oil;
 100 doz Cod Liver Oil;
 8000 lbs Epsom Salts;
 250 boxes Castile Soap;
 500 lbs Honduras Sarsaparilla;
 100 doz Metal Syringes;
 200 doz Glass Syringes;
 100 doz Rubber Syringes;
 200 doz Brandreth's Pills;
 150 doz Wright's Pills;
 100 doz Jayne's Expectorant;
 100 doz Dalley's Pain Extractor;
 100 doz Mustang Liniment;
 150 doz Opodeldoc;
 75 dox Ayer's Cherry Pectoral;
 250 doz Lyon's Insect Powders;
 200 doz Townsend's Sarsaparilla;
 300 doz Seidlitz Powders, &c., &c.,

Together with every other article in our line, comprising the largest and best assorted stock of Drugs, Patent Medicines, Perfumery and Fancy Goods, &c., to be found on this coast.

   CROWELL & CRANE,
    Wholesale Druggists,
  Corner of Front and Clay streets.

Wholesale druggists, like Crowell & Crane in San Francisco, provided drugstores and pharmacies with medicinal supplies, including patent medicines. Commission merchants that served the railroads also purchased from these companies and distributed the goods to the railroad camps.

Similar to today's over-the-counter drugs, patent medicines would not have required a formal doctor visit or written prescription. These popular medicines claimed to cure a host of maladies. Chinese railroad workers may have taken patent medicines in addition to or in place of herbal remedies that were harder to obtain. Chinese tonic wines and U.S.-produced bitters contained high levels of alcohol.

# 5
## Leisure

ANTAN GAMBLING, CANTON, PHOTO BY AH FONG

Building the Railroad

Adapting to a New Environment

Defining Identity

Health and Well-Being

Leisure

Leaving a Legacy

Appendices

# A Day's Job Well Done

Chinese railroad workers on the Central Pacific Railroad endured long hours of dangerous, backbreaking work. Workers may have chosen to spend their spare time socializing with their fellow countrymen, playing traditional games, gambling, relaxing with a smoke, or having a drink.

Gambling has been a prominent part of Chinese culture since as early as 2300 B.C. The world's earliest playing card comes from China and is dated to around the 11th century A.D.

Chinese gambling and gaming practices have fascinated scholars, such as 19th-century ethnographer Stewart Culin, who sketched and described games he observed the Chinese playing in Philadelphia.

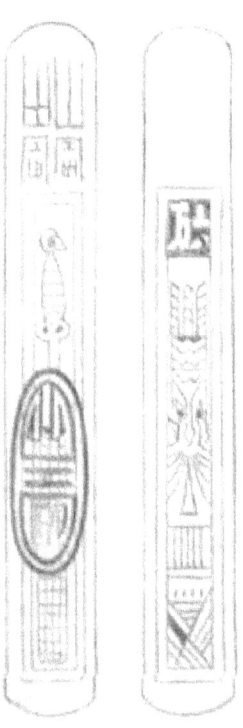

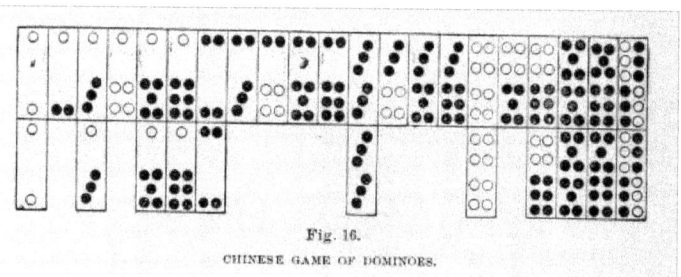

Fig. 16.
CHINESE GAME OF DOMINOES.

## Placing a Bet

Railroad workers carried few belongings with them, as they had to be able to pack up camp quickly and move to the next construction stop. The most popular gambling games were those that required few pieces, such as *fan-tan* and dice.

The game of *fan-tan* (translation: repeatedly spreading out) was a simple elimination game that involved betting on the odds of a certain number of game counters or cash (coins or other small objects) remaining after groups of four were removed. Although typically played on a small table using a wooden or tin square, called a "spreading-out square" and a "spreading-out rod," railroad workers could have used a flat area of ground or flat rock as their table and a stick as a "spreading-out rod."

Chinese dice were small cubes of bone incised with the numbers one through six—one number on each side. Dice ranged in size from a 1/10 in. to a 1/7 in. cube, and different sizes were employed for specific games, according to custom. One of the better known games was called *sanliu baozi* (three-six dice) or *sing luk*.

*Sing luk* was played by three players, using three dice. The goal of the game was to "out throw" the first player by making a higher cast. Stakes were paid to the player with the highest cast. Casts were ranked in the following order: (1) three sixes down; (2) four, five, six down; (3) two alike down; and (4) one, two, three down.

## Portable Games

*Weiqi* was also a popular game among the Chinese during the 19th century. It was relatively simple to set up and involved few gaming accessories. This game, too, was an opportunity for gambling. Glass gaming pieces have been found on many Chinese archaeological sites, including railroad camps.

*Weiqi* is a game of strategy that uses these small, glass gaming pieces to surround an opponent and prevent further play. When the game concludes, players count up their territories and the number of captured pieces to determine which of them has the most points.

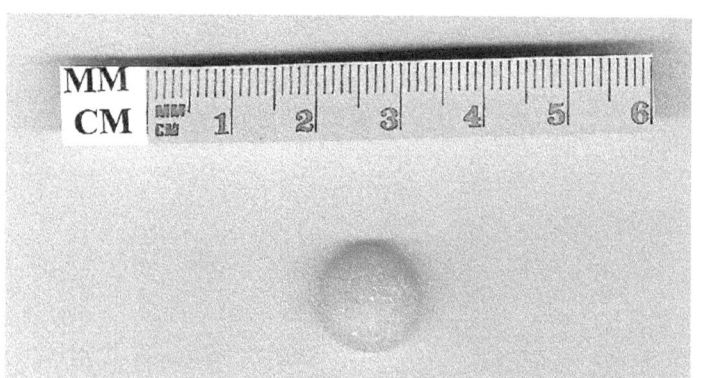

Glass gaming markers were approximately 1.1 cm in diameter and 0.5 cm in thickness. They were either "black" (black, dark green, brown, or blue) or "white" (white or off-white) in color.

Markers were also used in *fan-tan*. The black discs were called *hak chü* (black pearl) and were worth $1.00, while the white discs were called *pak chü* (white pearl) and were worth $5.00.

Coins also served as gambling tokens. Low-denomination Chinese, Vietnamese, and Japanese brass and zinc coins were used in various gambling games.

Archaeologists often assign specific categories to artifacts based on function or use. Researchers should keep in mind that people frequently reused or refashioned things into new objects to suit their needs. An example of this are these gaming pieces made from opium cans.

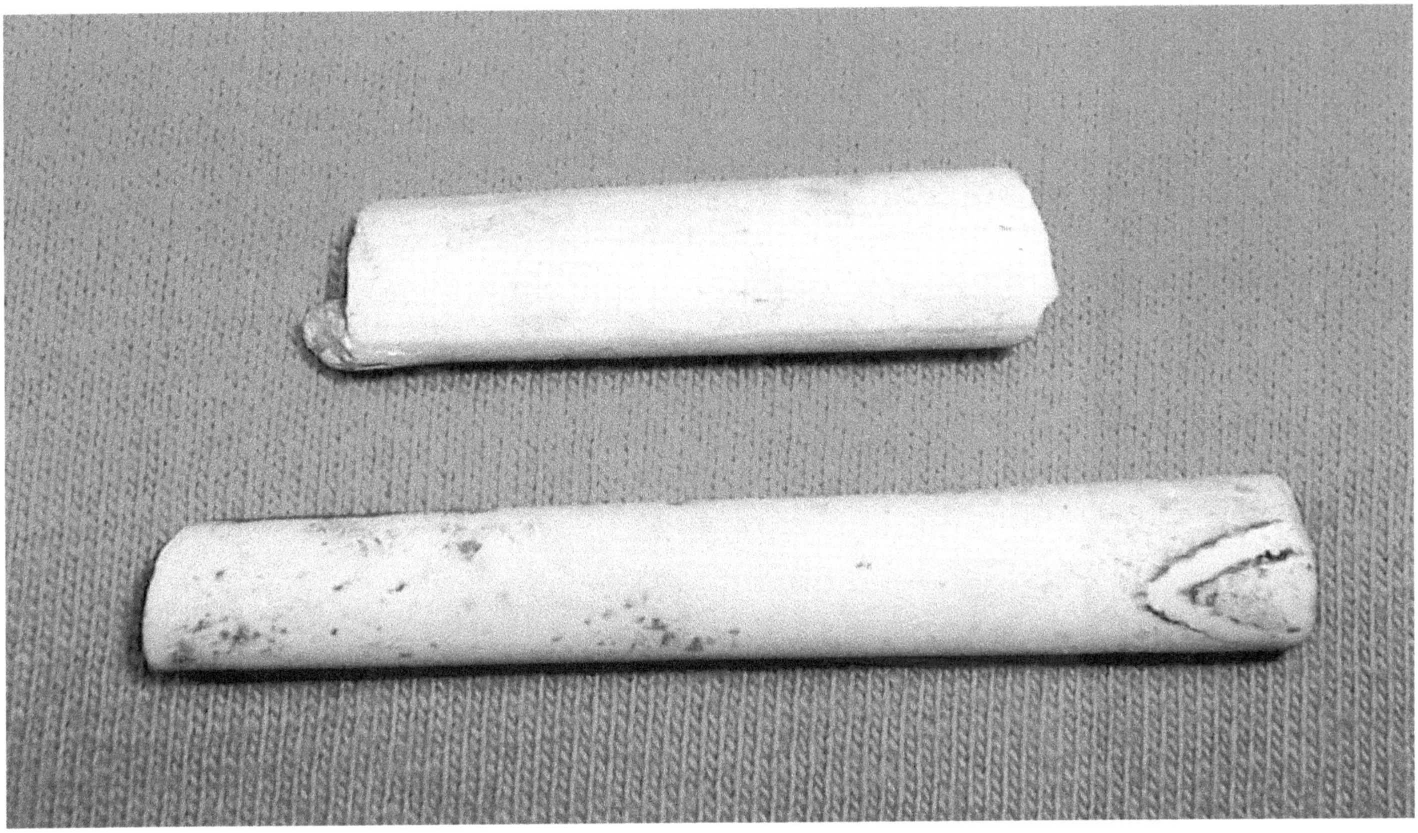

# Enjoying a Smoke

Some railroad workers also enjoyed smoking tobacco, either with a Chinese-made pipe or a locally available clay pipe. Both tobacco and opium smoking may have offered laborers a temporary escape from an often hostile environment, as well as a chance to socialize with fellow Chinese.

Chinese tobacco pipes are long and had a glass or bone mouthpiece, a wooden or bamboo body, and a brass bowl. The length of the pipe might be an indicator of the smoker's social status. If pipes were very long, the smokers would not be able to light the bowl by themselves, but would have needed others light it for them.

In the 19th century, solid kaolin (refined clay) tobacco pipes were mass-produced in Europe and imported into the United States. Fragments of these stems or bowls are common on archaeological sites, including Chinese railroad-worker sites like Summit Camp, the Windmill Tree site, and Matlin Section Station. Workers may have been using these pipes as a substitute for the Chinese-manufactured pipes, which were more expensive and difficult to obtain.

## Wine and Whiskey

Drinking was another way in which all railroad workers could relax after a hard day of work. Many container fragments found by archaeologists on Chinese railroad camp sites came from southern China, where the favored spirit was a potent alcoholic beverage made from either rice or sugarcane.

Some containers were stamped on the base with a mark indicating place of manufacture.

Both tiny and small cups were used to serve liquor. This tiny cup (about an inch high) is decorated in the Four Season Flower pattern. It was probably used to serve warm wine.

Liquor was also served in more refined vessels, such as this porcelain decanter decorated with a "Simple Flower" design motif. This vessel could also have held tea or sauce. At railroad camps like Summit Camp it is common to find small pieces of these vessels.

Fragments of glass wine and beer bottles are also commonly found at all camp sites, including those occupied by Chinese workers. American beer and French wine may have been easier to obtain than Chinese rice wine, which may have been reserved for special occasions.

# 6
# Leaving a Legacy

Building the Railroad

Adapting to a New Environment

Defining Identity

Health and Well-Being

Leisure

Leaving a Legacy

Appendices

## The Ten-Mile Day

After five years of labor, the race to the finish came at Promontory Summit in southern Utah. Charles Crocker, the financial backer of the Central Pacific Railroad, had made a $10,000 bet that his Chinese workforce could lay 10 miles of track in a single day, beating the East Coast–based Union Pacific crew record of 7.5 miles. By 1869, the Chinese workers had built the railroad through California and Nevada, and were an organized force used to long days of grueling, challenging labor. On April 28, in coordination with a small group of Irish rail handlers, Chinese laborers laid down 3,520 rails, connected by 55,000 spikes and 14,000 bolts, creating more than the 10 miles that Crocker had bet. The Chinese workers had proven themselves time and again, and had become a trusted and critical part of the railroad construction, working well with their bosses and Irish laborers. Yet, in the end, even on the day of triumph and at the celebration afterward, as well as in many subsequent historical accounts, the Chinese remained nameless—becoming, simply, "John Chinaman." The story of the Chinese laborers became only a footnote, as history remembered instead the triumph of a line that helped to link the East to the West.

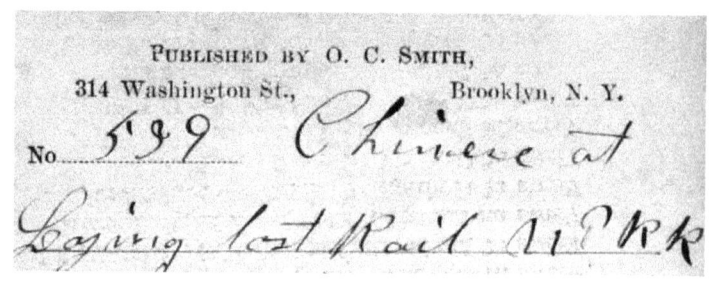

Three Chinese, based on clothing

### HONORS TO JOHN CHINAMAN.

Mr. Strowbridge, when work was all over, invited the Chinamen who had been brought over from Victory for the purpose, to dine in his boarding car. When they entered all the guests and officers present cheered them as the chosen representatives of the race which have greatly helped to build the road—a tribute they well deserved, and which evidently gave them much pleasure.

—*San Francisco Newsletter May 15, 1869*

*Fifty-nine years ago a squad of eight Irishmen and a small army of Chinese coolies made a record in track laying that has never been equaled. In one day, on April 28, 1869, these men, fired with the enthusiasm of the greatest railroad constructive race in the history of the world, laid ten miles and fifty-six feet of track in a little less than twelve hours to bring the railroad of the Central Pacific three and one-half miles from Promontory, Utah, where connection was made a few days later with the Union Pacific to form the first transcontinental railroad.*

*The names of the Irish rail handlers have been passed down through the years. Their super-human achievement will be remembered as long as there is railroad history. So, too, will that day's work of "John Chinaman" be recalled as the most stirring event in the building of the railroad.*

*—Erle Heath, Southern Pacific Bulletin, Vol. 16, No. 5, p. 3, May 1928*

Completion of the transcontinental railroad inspired construction efforts to connect every state west of the Mississippi, as well as Mexico and Canada. As experienced workers, Chinese were in high demand and migrated with the railroad-building operations. The archaeological record reflects this. Researchers have documented railroad camps associated with Chinese workers in southern California, Oregon, Nevada, Washington, Idaho, Montana, Utah, Arizona, and Texas.

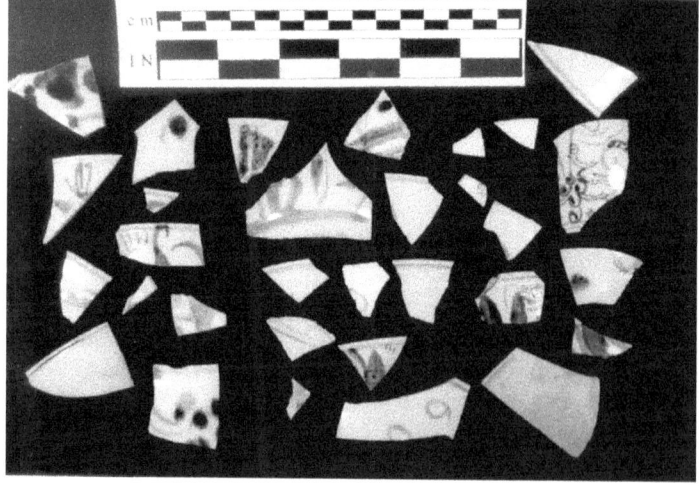

# Golden Spike National Historic Park

*—Michael R. Polk*

Promontory Summit lies in a cold, windswept, high-desert environment in rural northern Utah. It is a place set away from the urban population of the nearby Wasatch Front and lacks significant water resources. It remains sparsely populated 145 years after being the center of one of the most significant events to occur in the United States: the completion of the first transcontinental railroad. Such a feat had never been undertaken anywhere before. The achievement was not only a technological marvel, but had equally important social, political, and economic significance for the country and the world as a whole.

The area surrounding the location of the last spike was a place of the most intense construction activity undertaken from 1868 into 1869. It was where construction culminated, when the Union Pacific, from Omaha, and the Central Pacific, from Sacramento, met, and the railroads were joined in a grand celebration on May 10, 1869. The area

set aside as a national historic site in 1957 was designated the Golden Spike National Historic Site to commemorate the completion of the first transcontinental railroad and to acknowledge the tremendous historical consequences that occurred as a result. On July 30, 1965, it became part of the National Park System. The site was listed in the National Register of Historic Places in 1966, and its significance was documented for the register in 1986.

*TO COMMEMORATE THE CENTENNIAL OF THE FIRST TRANSCONTINENTAL RAILROAD IN AMERICA AND TO PAY TRIBUTE TO THE CHINESE WORKERS OF THE CENTRAL PACIFIC RAILROAD WHOSE INDOMITABLE COURAGE MADE IT POSSIBLE.*

*—Plaque placed by the Chinese Historical Society of America, 1969*

# History Silenced

*—Sue Lee*

The Chinese Historical Society of America is the oldest organization dedicated to preserving the legacy of Chinese in America in the country. Founded in 1963, when there were fewer than 300,000 Chinese in the United States, the organization set out to collect oral histories, preserve historic sites, collect artifacts, and memorialize significant milestones and achievements. May 10, 1969 marked the centennial of one of the most important infrastructure projects in American history—the completion of the first transcontinental railroad.

The moment had come for CHSA to place the role of the Chinese workers on the Central Pacific Railroad in perspective and reclaim their rightful position in the building of the American West.

CHSA initiated plans to ensure recognition. Two commemorative plaques were to be installed, one at each end of the Central Pacific, Sacramento and Promontory. Letters were sent to influential members of Congress to request their endorsement and inclusion of the Chinese at the centennial celebration. CHSA received a telegram from the Centennial Commission, stating that a "spokesman for the Chinee [sic] Community will be on Speakers platform for recognition and short speech presentation."

Upon arrival at the Golden Spike Ceremony in Promontory, Utah, on May 10, 1969, CHSA President Philip Choy was shocked that the plaque

presentation was not included in the official program. He listened as the keynote speaker, U.S. Labor Secretary Volpe stated, "Who else but Americans could drill ten tunnels in mountains thirty feet deep in snow? Who else but Americans could chisel through miles of solid granite?" Mr. Choy and his fellow delegates (including Col. John and Mrs. Mary Young) from San Francisco could not believe the lack of understanding and knowledge reflected in the statement.

After the program, the group was led to a small auditorium, with about 200 people, to dedicate the plaque. Thousands of other attendees were outside to see the Golden Spike reenactment and did not hear a word. Afterwards, the Chinese community strenuously decried the injustice of omitting any mention of the contribution of Chinese workers at this national event. But no one was listening.

The centennial organizers failed CHSA and the public and denied a true chapter in American history. But CHSA has never given up, and is dedicated as ever to ensuring that the labor of our pioneering ancestors is not forgotten, that our history is expressed in our own voices, in our own words, in our own way, that our history is embraced as an integral part of the American historical narrative, that Chinese helped build the American West.

# A Heritage of Discrimination

### —Connie Young Yu and Rebecca Allen

By the end of the 1870s, a nationwide depression affected the western states. Widespread unemployment and discontent cast dark shadows. The Southern Pacific Railroad, formerly known as the Central Pacific, was the largest landowner in the West and had become an empire. The "Octopus," as it was called, controlled the fates of farmers and small businessmen, squeezing them dry with high shipping rates. Small farmers were crushed by land monopoly, and state governments made regulations benefitting only the wealthy. Unemployed and dissatisfied white workers had an easy scapegoat for their troubles.

Anti-Chinese workers' groups had been in existence since the mid-1850s, inciting violence against Chinese in mining camps and city streets alike. As labor troubles brewed, they grew in size and number. By the 1870s organizations, such as the Anti-Coolie Association and the Supreme Order of the Caucasians, attempted to organize a boycott of Chinese labor throughout California. As the opposition to the use of Chinese labor became increasingly vociferous, Chinese were the victims of daily torments and organized outrages. Chinatowns from Denver to Los Angeles and north to Seattle were besieged with riots, murders, and fires.

On May 6, 1882, President Arthur signed the Chinese Exclusion Act, the only federal legislation in U.S. history to restrict the immigration of a people on the basis of race. Chinese laborers were prohibited from coming to the United States for ten years. Those already in the U.S. were permitted to leave and return only if they had re-entry permits. Merchants, teachers, students, and travelers could be admitted only through the strictest regulations. The act further stated that hereafter no Chinese could be naturalized as a citizen of the United States.

Archaeologists find indications of this racial hatred. The Market Street Chinatown in San Jose was destroyed by arson on May 4, 1887. From that archaeological site, recovered artifacts, such as burned wood and ceramic bowls, show evidence of that fire.

The Exclusion Act remained in place until 1943. While the first generations of Chinese Americans felt alienated, their children regarded the United States as their home.

## Archaeology and Preservation of Memory

Archaeological sites remain as testimony of the Chinese railroad-worker experience. Evidence from archaeological sites is critical to understanding the workers' experiences and the extent of their adaptation to new environments and challenges. Although archaeological sites seem long-lasting, they are fragile resources. Surfaces erode, modern construction and utility corridors impact archaeological sites, and well-intentioned visitors pick up valuable traces of the past as souvenirs. Every decade brings more impacts to the archaeological record and can further mute the voices of the past. Preservation of archaeological resources ensures that physical reminders of past memories and stories are brought forward to the future.

## Message on a Cliff Face in Montana

—*Kelly J. Dixon and Timothy R. Urbaniak*

Under construction by 1880, the Northern Pacific Railroad was the first railway to enter eastern Montana. On August 22, 1883, the Northern Pacific Railroad drove the last spike to complete the transcontinental mainline at Independence Creek, Montana Territory, about 50 miles west of Helena, and 30 miles west of the Continental Divide. A group of Chinese railroad workers competed with their Irish and Slavic counterparts to finish the last mile of track.

Thousands of Chinese laborers worked and lived in camps like this while constructing transcontinental railways throughout the American West, but few historical images of such camps survive. An artist created this drawing by integrating historical records and archaeological evidence to present a snapshot of work and life in the "Last Chance" Northern Pacific Railroad camp along the Clark Fork River in northwestern Montana. Archaeologists in Montana have found traces of many Chinese camps, traces that begin to give voice to the nameless railroad workers.

Numerous industries supported railroad expansion across the nation. Approximately 50 miles from the nearest transcontinental railroad (Northern Pacific), archaeologists noted a cliff face incised with Chinese characters. This inscription was found at a site associated with a coal-mining district in southeastern Montana. The initial translation suggests that these are traditional Chinese characters, translating to "Sun Ziqian was here August 29." Sun was the person's family name, and Ziqian was his given name.

Railroads were heavily dependent on coal as engine fuel. The fact that the only known Chinese inscription in Montana (and to the best of our knowledge, in the American West) is associated with a coal-mining site highlights the connection of Chinese laborers to coal industries and mining towns miles away from railroad rights-of-way. This inscription underscores the variety of ways in which Chinese labor was employed to support the railroads.

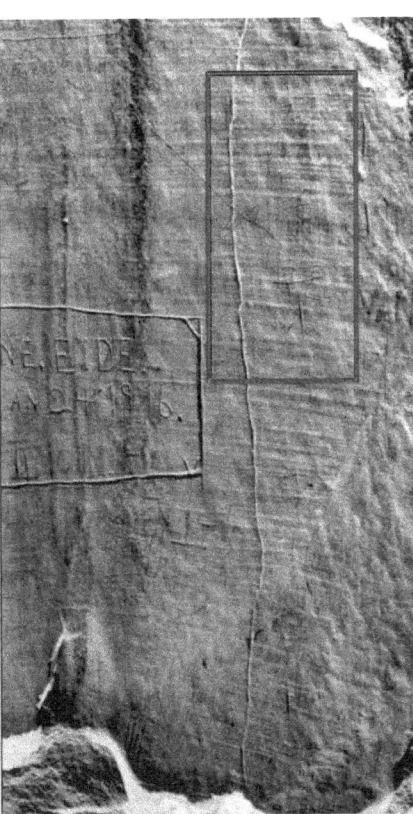

The image on the left is a closeup view of the Chinese inscription reading: "Sun Ziqian was here August 29." The image at the right shows the larger panel with adjacent non-Chinese inscriptions; this image is shown in negative image for legibility, and the Chinese characters are outlined by the rectangle.

# Old Ties and New Home Bases

A folk song from southern China expresses the feelings of a wife left behind in Guangdong:

> *Flowers shall be my headdress once again,*
>
> *For my dear husband will return soon from*
>
> *A distant shore.*
>
> *Ten long years did I wait*
>
> *Trying to remember his face*
>
> *As I toiled at my spinning wheel each*
>
> *Lonely night.*

Some workers went home to China when the labor was done, returning to families who had waited many years to see them. More stayed, facing discrimination and violence, but continued to support their families from afar. They found new work and forged new relationships in many of the Chinatowns that still dot the western landscape: San Francisco, San Jose, and Los Angeles, California; Lovelock, Carlin, and Winnemucca, Nevada; Portland, Oregon; Seattle, Washington; and Vancouver, British Columbia. They became new home bases, but also represented a legacy of segregation, as Chinese individuals and communities banded together to withstand daily harassment, violence, and hostile legislation. Despite prejudice and anti-Chinese legislation, Chinese American residents greatly contributed to the local and state economies and communities.

Today's Chinatowns are reminders of the perseverance of Chinese Americans. The legacy of Chinese railroad-worker history and their new home bases can be found throughout the western United States. San Francisco was the main port at which most workers first arrived and has one of the West's most famous Chinatowns. It remains a vibrant presence and reminder of how the past has shaped the present.

# Descendant Voices

### —Connie Young Yu

There are many descendants of Chinese railroad workers in the United States. My great-grandfather, Lee Wong Sang, was one of the workers recruited by the Central Pacific in 1866. He came over to America, a 19-year-old villager from Taishan, to work on the "Iron Road." I know this because my grandfather, his son, told his daughter, my mother. And she told it to me. My family, like many descendants, has a paper trail of our ancestors. Some went back to China, and more either returned to the United States or never left.

Chinese immigrants to California faced extreme adversity and discrimination, but they endured.

I imagine Chinese workers, such as my great-grandfather, laboring to build Summit Tunnel by hand through the granite mountain, drilling inches a day.

William Temcuseh Sherman once said that if the railroad was ever built, it would be the work of giants. They did incredible, monumental work. The courage of the Chinese worker in doing what many thought was impossible has been largely omitted from history. But now we have the opportunity to set the record straight. We have a new awareness through the oral history of descendants, along with archaeological and historical research. I think that finally, Chinese workers will have their rightful place in American history.

Of those who returned to China, they took with them skills learned here and dreams of building an iron road in their native land. The Sunning (or Sun Ning) railway in Guangdong, China, was founded in 1906 by Chin Gee Hee, a former railroad worker and agent for the Great Northern Railway in Washington State. The railway was funded by overseas Chinese.

# Chinese Railroad Workers in North America Project

*—Gordon H. Chang, Shelley Fisher Fishkin, and Barbara L. Voss*

The Chinese Railroad Workers in North America Project seeks to give a voice to the Chinese migrants whose labor on the transcontinental railroad helped to shape the physical and social landscape of the American West. The project coordinates research in North America and Asia in order to create an online digital archive available to all, along with books, digital visualizations, conferences, and public events.

2015 marks the 150th anniversary of the introduction of large numbers of Chinese workers on the construction of the first transcontinental railway across North America. May 10, 2019 is the 150th anniversary of Leland Stanford's driving the famous "golden spike" to connect the Central Pacific and Union Pacific at Promontory Summit, Utah, to complete the line. The labor of these Chinese workers (who eventually numbered between 10,000 and 12,000 at any one moment) was central to creating the wealth that Leland Stanford used to found Stanford University. But these workers have never received the attention they deserve. We need to know how they contributed to shaping not just the physical, but the social landscape of

the West. The sesquicentennial anniversaries of the railroad's construction and completion provide an unprecedented opportunity to launch a major evaluation of their experiences.

Historians and other scholars in a range of disciplines in North America and in Asia are cooperating in locating new historical materials and developing a multidisciplinary approach to understanding and appreciating this long-neglected history. (Although the focus of the project is the Chinese railroad workers, the project also opens out into the lives these individuals lived during the decades after the railroad was completed.) In addition to recovering an unjustly neglected chapter of history of special significance for Stanford University, this transnational, collaborative, multiyear research project will pioneer in modeling new ways of exploring the shared past of China and the United States.

For more information, please see the web site at http://web.stanford.edu/group/chineserailroad/cgi-bin/wordpress/.

*In early 2015, the Society for Historical Archaeology published a special thematic issue of its journal, Historical Archaeology, entitled: The Archaeology of Chinese Railroad Workers in North America. The journal issue was developed from a Stanford University workshop in October 2013, sponsored and organized by the Chinese Railroad Workers in North America Project.*

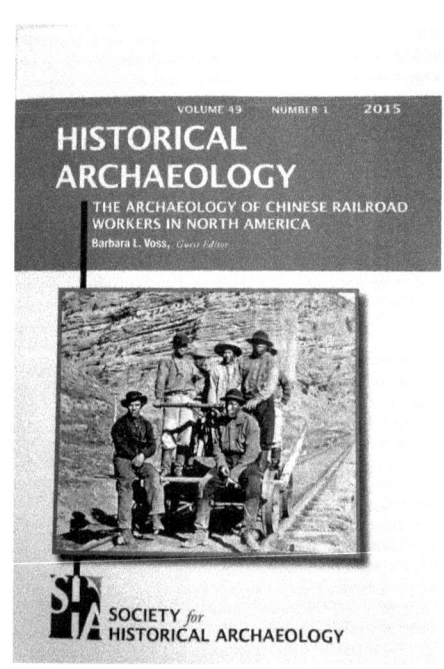

## CHSA Dedication to the Chinesee Railroad-Worker Legacy

In 2014, the Chinese Historical Society of America launched an initiative to commemorate the 145th anniversary of the completion of the first transcontinental railroad in the United States. That year witnessed unprecedented nationwide recognition, culminating in the U.S. Department of Labor inducting Chinese railroad workers into the Labor Hall of Honor. This occasion presented an opportunity to change the historical narrative. Descendants of railroad-worker families, along with CHSA, attended to honor the memory and legacy of their pioneer forefathers. With this historic occasion, CHSA launched a new chapter by sharing the stories of the descendants of known Chinese railroad workers who helped to build the American West.

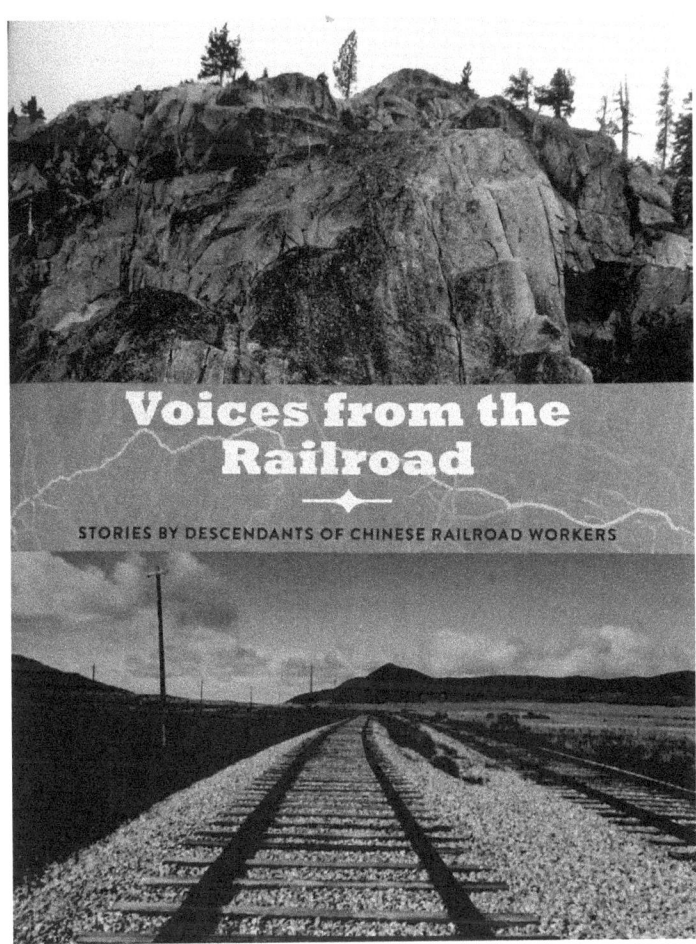

# 7
# Appendices

Building the Railroad

Adapting to a New Environment

Defining Identity

Health and Well-Being

Leisure

Leaving a Legacy

Appendices

# *Photo Captions and Credits*

## *The Strength of Collaboration*

Diorama at the California State Railroad Museum, showing railroad workers at Donner Summit. (Photo by Rebecca Allen, 2007)

## *Why Archaeology?*

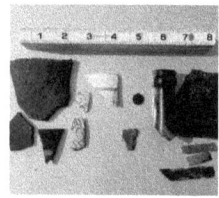

Artifacts from Summit Camp, displayed on an archaeologist's clipboard. (Photo by R. Scott Baxter, 2007)

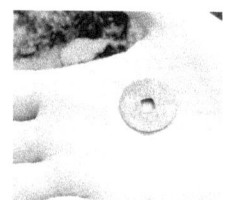

Rebecca Allen holding a Chinese coin from Summit Camp. (Photo by Chris McClellan, 2014)

## *Artist's Preface*

Certificate of Residence for Jim King (Jow Kee), 1894. (Courtesy of Connie Young Yu and Chinese Historical Society of America)

Portrait illustration. (Drawing by Amber Rankin, 2016)

## *1. Building the Railroad*

### Divider

Artifacts scattered on the ground surface in Utah. (Photo by Chris Merritt, 2014)

### Beginnings

William Evans at Summit Camp, 1967. (Courtesy of Paul Chace)

# The Engineer's Vision

 Theodore Judah, 1843. (California State Library)

 Mark Hopkins, 1886. (Photo by I. W. Taber, California State Library)

 Leland Stanford, 1864. (*Harper's Weekly*, January 23, 1864)

 Collis Potter Huntington, 1888. (Henry Clew, *28 Years in Wall Street*, https://archive.org/details/twentyeightyear00clew)

 Charles Crocker, 1888. (Henry Clew, *28 Years in Wall Street*, https://archive.org/details/twentyeightyear00clew)

# Bridging the Gap

 Levee at Sacramento looking north from a steamer to the railyard with Central Pacific Railroad (CPRR) cars in the background, about 1865–1867. (Stanford University, Alfred Hart Photograph Collection, nj339gb1246_05_0042)

 Front elevation of the north end of the Union Pacific Railroad works, Omaha, Nebraska, about 1867. (Photo by John Carbutt, Chicago, Union Pacific Railroad photo archive, SRC-7-2 Omaha Carbutt stereo.jpg)

 Summits of the Sierras 8,000–10,000 feet altitude, about 1865-1867. (Stanford University, Alfred Hart Photograph Collection, nj339gb1246_05_0042)

 Railroads in the United States in 1865, showing the Civil War railroad buildup in the East and the few rail lines west of the Mississippi. (Map and textual analysis, Stanford University, and Will Thomas, University of Nebraska, Lincoln, 2016)

 Building the Union Pacific Railroad through Nebraska, 1867. (Woodcut by Alfred R. Waud, reproduced on page 567 of Albert D. Richardson, *Beyond the Mississippi*)

## Bridging the Gap (continued)

Promontory Point in 2014, looking west from the "Driving of the Golden Spike" site. (Photo adapted from original by Dennis Mook, 2016)

End of the track, Humboldt Plains, Nevada, taken during construction, about 1867. (Photo by Alfred Hart, Library of Congress, LC-1s00618v)

## Recruiting the Crews

Map of China showing the southern provinces that were home to many of the CPRR workers. (Drawing adapted by Amber Rankin, 2016)

Most of the railroad workers traveled to San Francisco from counties in Guangdong. (Drawing adapted by Amber Rankin, with the assistance of Clement Lai, from Philip Choy, *Canton Footprints*, 2016)

Hong Kong harbor, about 1870. (Photo by G. E. Morrison, *Album of Hongkong, Canton, Macao, Amoy and Foochow*)

Chinese on board the steamship *Alaska* on their way to San Francisco. (*Harper's Weekly*, April 29, 1876)

Advertisement in the *Pacific Coast Railroad Gazetteer*, 1870. (California State Library, California History Room, HEC2727.R34)

## By the Sweat of Their Brows

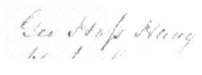
Chinese companies and individuals listed in the CPRR payroll records, about 1867. (California State Railroad Museum Archives)

Building the Siskiyou Railroad in Oregon, California, 1886. (Oregon Historical Society, Bb009945)

Hard at work excavating one of the Summit tunnels, CPRR. (*Harper's Weekly*, 1867)

Chinese workers drilling in the cut near Monterey, 1889. (California State Library, 001389203)

Chinese laborers at work. (Drawing by Amber Rankin, 2016)

Camp No. 28 payroll records listing Chinese blacksmith and helpers, 1866. (California State Railroad Museum Archives)

# Tools of the Trade

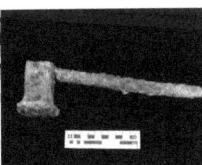

Sledgehammers, both with long and short handles, have been recovered in maintenance stations, yards, and work sites along the CPRR. They were essential for breaking rocks and were a part of the blacksmith's toolkit. This example was found in a blacksmith forge in the CPRR railyard in Folsom, California. (Photo by PAR Environmental Services, Inc., 2012)

Shovels have been documented at many work camps and maintenance stations along the CPRR. This example was recovered from a campsite east of Summit Camp in the high Sierra Nevada Mountains. (Photo by John Molenda, 2015)

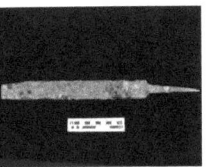

Files were necessary tools used along the railroad and are found at nearly every work camp. This example was recovered at the railyard in Folsom, California. (Photo by PAR Environmental Services, Inc., 2012)

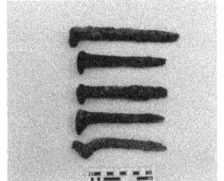

Spikes occur at every railroad construction camp, site, and railroad station and yard. These examples were recovered from excavations at the CPRR machine shops and foundry site in Folsom. (Photo by PAR Environmental Services, Inc., 2011)

Lithographs tracked the progress of the CPRR during its construction and depicted Chinese laborers breaking up rocks with picks and sledgehammers at the Donner Summit tunnels. (*Harper's Weekly*, 1867)

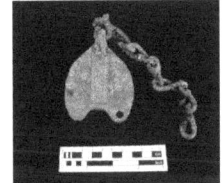

CPRR lock found at the site of the 1868–1881 engine house in Folsom's railyard. A similar lock stamped with CPRR was found at Watercress Maintenance Station in Utah. (Photo by PAR Environmental Services, Inc., 2013)

Illustration of the CPRR lock showing the company name stamped on the brass. (Drawing by Amber Rankin, 2013)

# The Donner Summit Tunnels

Interior view of one of the Donner Summit tunnels. (Photo by Adrianna Allen, 2014)

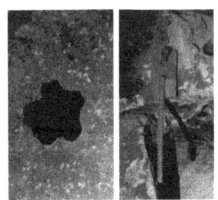

Drilling hardware and a drill hole left behind from the construction of a Donner Summit tunnel. (Photos by Adrianna Allen, 2014)

Interior view of one of the Donner Summit tunnels before completion, about 1867. (Photo by Alfred Hart, California State Library)

Modern-day graffiti found inside a Donner Summit tunnel, acknowledging the work of the Chinese railroad worker. (Photos by Adrianna Allen, 2014)

## The Indispensable Help

While there are photographs and drawings of the men who served as laborers on the railroad line, no images have been found of the many Chinese who provided support services to both Chinese and non-Chinese camps. This drawing is based on a late 19th-century photograph of a Chinese cook in a logging camp, but is likely similar to the attire and tools used by Chinese cooks during railroad construction. (Drawing by Amber Rankin, 2016)

Chinese grooms tending the horses and supply wagons at Owl Gap Cut. This cut was 80 miles from Sacramento and, when finished, was 900 ft. long and 45 ft. deep, about 1867. (Photo by Alfred Hart, Library of Congress, Lot 11477, LC-1s0049lr)

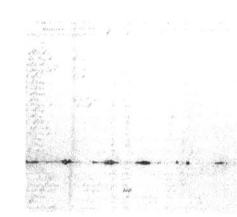

Camp No. 51 payroll records listing a Chinese night cook and waiters, 1866. (California State Railroad Museum Archives)

# 2. Adapting to a New Environment

## Divider

Archaeologists R. Scott Baxter and Sarah Heffner with filmmaker Laurence Campling at the Summit Camp site. (Photo by Chris McClellan, 2014)

## New Landscapes

Modern-day Guangdong, a land of water and greenery. (Photo by Barbara L. Voss, 2014)

View of Donner Lake from Donner Summit with snow sheds in the foreground, 1868. (Photo by Andrew J. Russell, Library of Congress, http://loc.gov/pictures/resource/cph.3g11400/)

## The Camps

The tent camps became portable homes for the men. This drawing depicts typical activities in camps, as interpreted from lithographs, newspaper accounts, and archaeological evidence from features and artifacts. (Drawing by Amber Rankin, 2016)

# Changing Shelters

CPRR construction route, showing camps along the way. (Drawing by Amber Rankin, 2015)

Tents remained the prevailing form of housing for the Chinese men at Promontory Point in Utah. (Stanford University, Alfred Hart Photograph Collection, nj339gb1246_05_0310)

In the desert workers were housed in tents, about 1867. The larger tent likely was used for communal meals and the kitchen. (Stanford University, Alfred Hart Photograph Collection, nj339gb1246_05_0321)

Sacramento's Chinese district provided temporary housing for workers as they prepared to join the CPRR construction crews in the Sierra, about 1950. (California State Archives)

# Rock, Wood, and Metal

East portal of Summit Tunnel and the Wagon Road from Tunnel No. 7, showing cabins at Summit Camp. (Photo by Alfred Hart, Library of Congress, LC-1s00548v)

Remains of a hearth at Summit Camp. (Photo by R. Scott Baxter, 2007)

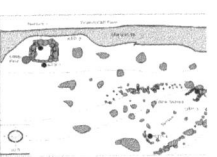
Archaeological site map, Summit Camp site. (Drawing by R. Scott Baxter, 2007)

Artifacts and modern debris scattered on the surface at the Summit Camp site. (Photo by Chris McClellan, 2014)

# Canvas, Sticks, and Cooling Pits

End of track near Humboldt Lake, about 1867. (Photo by Alfred Hart, Library of Congress, LC-1s00618v)

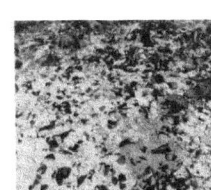
Artifacts scattered on the surface near Monument Rock in Utah. (Photo by Chris Merritt, 2014)

Today the old, abandoned route of the CPRR stretches across the Nevada and Utah deserts as far as the eye can see. (Photo by Chris Merritt, 2014)

Archaeologists document features, such as this depression in the desert sand, where a Chinese worker would have slept to keep cool. This feature is near an old railroad grade in Utah. (Photo by Chris Merritt, 2014)

## Canvas, Sticks, and Cooling Pits (continued)

Remnants of the juniper branches from A-frame tents are visible on the landscape in the old camps. This frame protects a shallow depression where the worker once slept along the CPRR grade in Nevada. (Photo by G. J. "Chris" Graves, CPRR archives, 2005)

## Dressing the Part

Suspender and stocking clasps and belt buckles are also found in small numbers at Chinese construction camps, attesting to the workers' blending of traditional and locally available garb. (Drawings by Amber Rankin, 2015)

Chinese railroad workers with rubber boots and leather boots, traditional tunics and hats, and American pants, 1889. (California State Library, Image 001389203)

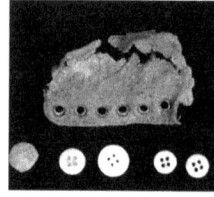

Remnants of leather boots, some with rivets, have been recovered in Folsom, Summit Camp, Carlin, and other railroad camps or maintenance yards. (Photo by PAR Environmental Services, Inc., 2011)

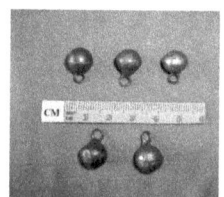

These ball-shaped shirt buttons were manufactured in China and are visible in historical photos on Chinese tunics. They are often recovered at the campsites. This example is from a Northern Pacific Railroad campsite in Montana. (Photo by Gary Weisz, 2014)

This fragment of a boot heel was recovered from the CPRR yard in Folsom. (Photo by PAR Environmental Services, Inc., 2011)

Buttons from the Summit Camp site hint at workers wearing non-traditional shirts, pants, and, perhaps, long underwear to keep warm in the winter months. (Photo by R. Scott Baxter, 2014)

Small fragments of rubber-coated canvas or leather have been found at high-elevation camps like Summit Camp. A search of catalogs produced by Sears Roebuck and other stores indicated that rubberized boots were available and likely were used in winter to keep feet dry during the tunnel-building efforts. (Drawing by Tammara Norton, reconstruction of a boot from an archaeological site, 1984)

Archaeologists rely on mercantile and retail store catalogs to identify the bits and pieces of clothing and footwear found on sites. Advertised as "Miner's Boots," these sturdy boots were made to withstand hard labor and adverse conditions. Historic photographs of Chinese workers indicate that similar footwear was worn by the laborers. (Montgomery Ward & Co.'s Catalogue No. 57, page 518, 1895)

## Stretching the Budget

Artifact scatter at Summit Camp site. (Photo by Chris McClellan, 2014)

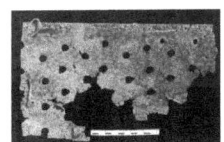

Can or sheet metal adapted for reuse by punching holes in the metal. This example is from a Chinese camp along a railroad east of Folsom. Similar examples have been recovered at Summit Camp and Chinese camps around Truckee. (Photo by Robert Hicks, 1995)

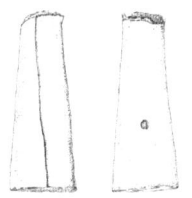

Rolled sheets of metal for use as funnels or other purposes have been found at a Chinese camp along a railroad east of Folsom and at Chinese camps outside Truckee, California. (Drawing by Tammara Norton, 1995)

Catfish. (Drawing adapted from El Dorado Trout Unlimited, *EDT News*, Summer 2014)

# 3. Defining Identity

## Divider

Commemorative plaque in Colfax celebrating the contributions of Chinese railroad workers. (Photo by Chris McClellan, 2014)

## Finding the Past

Chinese porcelain fragment on the ground at Donner's Pass. (Photo by Sarah Heffner, 2014)

A depression outlined by discarded rocks, this feature from Bovine, Utah, in the Great Salt Lake Desert contained a scatter of Chinese artifacts. (Photo by Kenneth Cannon, 2015)

Chinese work camp near Truckee, California, used by workers chopping wood for the railroad effort. (Photo by Sharon Waechter, 2010)

Site 42BO1134, Chinese worker camp on edge of the Central Pacific grade near Promontory Point. (Photo by Michael Polk, 2015)

## Pecked Marks on a Bowl

Peck mark that transliterates to "*xing*," from Summit Camp. (Photo by R. Scott Baxter, 2014)

Peck mark from Folsom that transliterates "treasure" or "Zhen" (woman's first name). (Photo by PAR Environmental Services, Inc., 2011)

## Pecked Marks on a Bowl (continued)

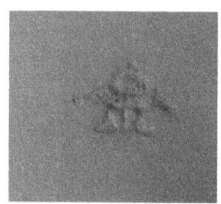
Peck mark from the Chinese community adjacent to the CPRR railyard in Folsom means "gold" or "*jin*." (Photo by PAR Environmental Services, Inc., 2011)

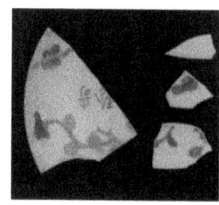
Peck mark on sherds recovered from Folsom that transliterates to "rare treasure." (Photo by PAR Environmental Services, Inc., 2011)

## Cooking the Chinese Way

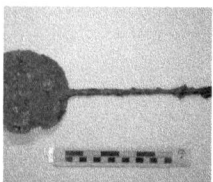
Long-handled, flat-blade spatulas, like this one recovered from Folsom, were typically used to stir food while cooking in cast-iron woks. (Photo by PAR Environmental Services, Inc., 2011)

Chinese eating a meal while fish are cooking in wok. (Drawing by Amber Rankin, 2016)

Fragments of cast-iron woks or heavy cooking pots have been recovered at Chinese construction camps along the Northern Pacific Railroad, Sacramento Valley Railroad in Folsom, camps near Truckee, and at Summit Camp. (Photo by PAR Environmental Services, Inc., 2011)

Hairpin hearth from the Selkirk site. (Photo by Julia Costello, 1998)

Sketch of the hearth from the Selkirk site. (Drawing by Julia Costello, 1998)

Chinese cleavers are distinctive in shape and have a Chinese identification mark stamped into the blade (often not visible on rusted examples found on sites). The cleaver shown here is from the Folsom Chinese community, which was across the street from the CPRR yard. Examples have also been found at Lake View Camp on the Virginia-Truckee Railroad, CPRR's Summit Camp, and at the Southern Pacific Camp in Langtry, Texas. (Photo by PAR Environmental Services, Inc., 2011)

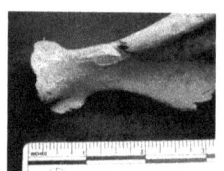
Cleavers leave a distinctive V-shaped notch on bones. This pig bone recovered in Folsom has this distinctive cleaver mark. (Photo by PAR Environmental Services, Inc., 2011)

## Comfort Food

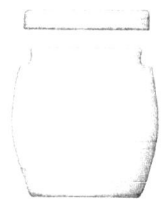
Barrel-jar fragments have been found at nearly every camp along the CPRR occupied by Chinese and attest to the importation of traditional foodstuffs. (California State Parks, 1984)

Towns along the railroad often had Chinese-owned businesses that supplied traditional imported foodstuffs to the workers. Archaeologists rely on the advertisements placed in local newspapers to ascertain the availability of comfort food. (*Truckee Republic*, 1875)

## Comfort Food (continued)

The lips, spouts, and bases of soy-sauce containers have been identified at Summit Camp, China Kitchen, Bovine, Promontory Point, and other sites along the CPRR in Nevada and Utah. (California State Parks, 1984)

Shouldered jars came in many sizes and are also found at nearly all camps studied by archaeologists. (California State Parks, 1984)

Fragments of these small, squat jars have been found at numerous Chinese-occupied camps along the Central Pacific. While other storage jars had lids that fit over the lip, in this example the lid was set inside the rolled lip of the jar and secured with twine or rope, sealing the contents. (California State Parks, 1984)

The barrel jars (*back row*), green ginger jar (*center*), liquor bottle (*front left*), soy bottle (*front row, second from right*), and small and large jars have all been recovered from railroad construction camps. (Photo by PAR Environmental Services, Inc., 2011)

## A Bowl for Every Man

This drawing depicts the Double Happiness porcelain pattern. This pattern is most commonly found at sites occupied before 1870, such as Summit Camp and China Kitchen. (California State Parks, 1984)

Map of China depicting the general area known for the manufacture of folkware vessels. (Map adapted by Amber Rankin, 2016)

Chinese ceramic fragments from Seco, Utah, including a liquor bottle spout (*top*), and Bamboo pattern bowl (*middle*). (Photo from Anan S. Raymond and Richard Fike, *Rails East to Promontory*, 1981)

These fragments of Double Happiness bowls were photographed at a railroad construction camp in the high Sierra. (Photo by John Molenda, 2014)

This bowl is decorated with the Bamboo pattern, the most common pattern found on sites dating about 1869 and later. (California State Parks, 1984)

## Serving Soups and Sauces

Map of China depicting the general location of kilns and potters that produced Winter Green (celadon) and Four Season Flower wares. (Map adapted by Amber Rankin, 2016)

Winter Green (also called celadon) rice-bowl base from a Chinese camp along the CPRR grade in Utah. (Photo by Kenneth Cannon, 2015)

## Serving Soups and Sauces (continued)

Winter Green bowl sketch. Winter Green patterned bowls, cups, and spoons have blue marks on their bases and have been found at many camps investigated by archaeologists in California, Nevada, and Utah. (California State Parks, 1984)

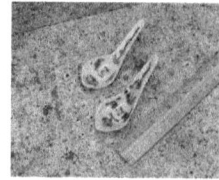

The Four Season Flower pattern has been found on spoons, tiny cups, and a variety of bowls at Summit Camp and other sites along the railroad in Nevada and Utah. (Photo by G. J. "Chris" Graves, 2005)

While not as common as Bamboo or Double Happiness, the Four Season Flower pattern occurs in small numbers on many of the construction campsites along the CPRR grade, including Summit Camp and Carlin. (California State Parks, 1984)

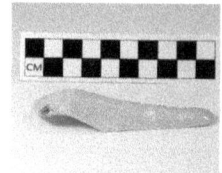

Fragment of a Winter Green soup spoon from a Chinese cap along the CPRR grade in Utah. (Photo by Kenneth Cannon, 2015)

## A Popular Import

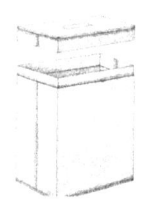

Opium tins were made of brass, of uniform size and shape, and are recovered at all camps. (California State Parks, 1984)

These opium tins were recovered from a camp at Bovine, Utah. (Photo by Kenneth Cannon, 2015)

Map of China showing the common origins of opium exported to the United States. (Map adapted by Amber Rankin, 2016)

Opium-can lid with Li Yun cartouche found at the Ombey station camp, Utah. (Photo by Kenneth Cannon, 2014)

Opium cans with remnants of paper labels survive on sites with favorable soil and climate conditions. This example was recovered from the Chinese community next to the CPRR yards in Folsom. (Photo by PAR Environmental Services, Inc., 2011)

This cartouche transliterates to Li Yun, a brand of opium popular during the 19th century and found on many Chinese sites, including railroad camps. (California State Parks, 2015)

## More Evidence of the Familiar

Chinese coin from a Northern Pacific Railroad camp west of Noxon, Montana. Many of this type of coin have been recovered at CPRR sites, including Summit Camp. (Photo by Gary Weitz, 2015)

These coins were found at an 1869 stone railroad culvert near Promontory Point. (Photo by Michael Polk, 2015)

Chinese liquor bottles are also common on the sites once used by Chinese laborers. This representative example provides detail of the flared lip and bulbous body that characterizes these containers. (California State Parks, 1984)

Chinese oil lamps, such as this one, have been found at railroad camps, including archaeological sites in the high Sierra region. They were lit by filling the middle well with peanut or other oil and placing a wick in the oil. (Photo by PAR Environmental Services, Inc., 2011)

Chinese medicine vials like this example have been recorded at every construction camp occupied by Chinese along the CPRR, as well as at Northern Pacific and Southern Pacific railroad camps. (Photo by PAR Environmental Services, Inc., 2011)

This liquor-bottle fragment was recovered from a camp along the CPRR grade in Utah. (Photo by Kenneth Cannon, 2015)

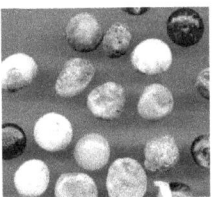

Glass gaming pieces from a Truckee Chinese woodcutting camp. (Photo by Sharon Waechter, 2010)

## *4. Health and Well-Being*

### Divider

Statue of Chinese railroad workers in San Luis Obispo, California, dedicated in 2003. (Photo by Rebecca Allen, 2016)

### Hazards of the Job

Chinese line camp at Brown's Station, near Lovelock, Nevada, about 1869. (Photo by Alred Hart, Library of Congress Prints and Images Online, LC-DIG-stereo-1s00615)

"Work on the Last Mile of the Pacific Railroad—Mingling of European with Asiatic Laborers." (Library of Congress Prints and Images Online, LC-USZ62-127764)

# Hazards of the Job (continued)

Article about an avalanche near Donner Summit from *Marysville Daily Appeal*, 1866. (California Digital Newspaper Collection, Center for Bibliographic Studies and Research, University of California, Riverside)

Article from the *Sacramento Daily Union*, June 30, 1870, discussing bones of deceased Chinese workers being taken to a private cemetery. (California Digital Newspaper Collection, Center for Bibliographic Studies and Research, University of California, Riverside)

Identity brick from the Chinese cemetery in Carlin, Nevada. (Photo by Sue Fawn Chung and John Joseph Crandall, 2014)

# Ancient and Effective

Dried gecko on display in the Kam Wah Chung Store in John Day, Oregon. Geckos are used in many Chinese medicinal preparations. (Photo by Sarah Heffner, 2009)

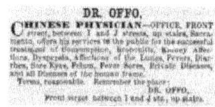

Dr. Offo's medicine ad appeared in the *Sacramento Daily Union*, March 1, 1860. (California Digital Newspaper Collection, Center for Bibliographic Studies and Research, University of California, Riverside)

Advertisement directed at Chinese for shipping freight via the Central Pacific Railroad. (Bancroft Library University of California, Berkeley, BANC PIC 1963.002:1829-A)

# Easing Aches and Pains

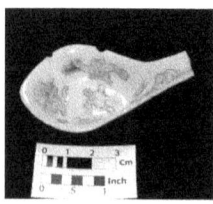

Soup spoon with Four Season Flower motif recovered from Chinatown in Folsom. Fragments of a soup spoon with this design have also been found at a railroad camp in Eureka County, Nevada. (Photo by PAR Environmental Services, Inc., 2014)

Chinese and Vietnamese coins from Noxon Line Camp, along the Northern Pacific Railroad in Montana. (Photo by Gary Weisz, 2014)

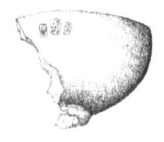

This opium pipe-bowl fragment was recovered from a Chinese work camp near the railyards at Folsom. Note the characters impressed into the clay. (Drawing by Tammara Norton, 1994)

# Healthy Habits

Chinese braiding a queue. (Drawing by Amber Rankin, 2016)

California Powder Works black-powder can found on the riverside of the Cabinet rock cut, Bonner County, Idaho. (Photo by Gary Weisz, 2014)

Representative sample of Chinese toothbrushes from Folsom. (Photo by PAR Environmental Services, Inc., 2011)

# Soup and Tea

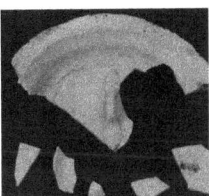
Fragment of a lid from a possible herbal steamer recovered from Folsom. (Photo by PAR Environmental Services, Inc., 2011)

Fragment of a base and spout from a possible herbal steamer, recovered from an archaeological site in Folsom. (Photo by PAR Environmental Services, Inc., 2011)

Man drinking tea by a hearth with an herbal steamer. (Drawing by Amber Rankin, 2016)

Representative example of a decorative Chinese teapot from the Chinatown adjacent to the CPRR railroad yard in Folsom. Fragments of decorative teapots have been found on several Chinese railroad-worker sites. (Photo by PAR Environmental Services, Inc., 2011)

Stoneware jug found at a Chinese camp next to the original CPRR grade near Beowawe, Nevada. It likely held water or tea. (Photo by G. J. "Chris" Graves, 2007)

Tea carrier heading east from the opening of Tunnel No. 8, Donner Summit, about 1867. (Photo by Alfred Hart, Library of Congress, LC-USZ62-50457)

# Internal Medicine

Chinese medicine vial from Terrace, Utah, the site of a former section camp for the Salt Lake Division of the CPRR. (Courtesy of Anan Raymond, 1981)

Liquor-bottle lip from a CPRR section station in Utah. (Photo by Kenneth Cannon, 2015)

## Internal Medicine (continued)

Chinese medicine bottle from Bovine, Utah, which served as a CPRR section station from 1869 to 1905. (Photo by Kenneth Cannon, 2015)

Cuttlefish-bone fragments from Lovelock Chinatown, Nevada. Though not yet documented on a Chinese railroad-worker site, cuttlefish was a popular food item and was likely provided to workers by Chinese merchants who supplied the railroad. (Nevada State Museum, Carson City, Nevada Department of Tourism and Cultural Affairs, 2010)

## Expanding the Traditional Medicine Kit

Advertisement by Crowell & Crane, wholesale druggists, in the *Daily Alta California* 12 (140), May 20, 1860. (California Digital Newspaper Collection, Center for Bibliographic Studies and Research, University of California, Riverside)

Advertisement for Dr. Hostetter's Celebrated Stomach Bitters in the *Los Angeles Herald*, April 24, 1883. (California Digital Newspaper Collection, Center for Bibliographic Studies and Research, University of California, Riverside)

Amethyst-colored patent-medicine bottle fragments from a Chinese railroad-worker site in Tahoe National Forest. (Photo by John Molenda, 2014)

Druggist's token found at Summit Camp. Druggists and other merchants used tokens to advertise their businesses. This token was produced by J. L. Polhemus, who operated a drugstore in Sacramento from the 1850s to the 1870s. (Photo by Paul Chace, 2014)

# 5. Leisure

## Divider

Chinese playing *fan-tan* in Canton, Kwangtung Province, China. (Library of Congress, LC-USZ62-80213

## A Day's Job Well Done

Chinese playing *fan-tan* on a makeshift table. (Drawing by Amber Rankin, 2016)

Sketch of Chinese cards from Stewart Culin's "The Gambling Games of the Chinese in America." (Drawing by Stewart Culin, 1891)

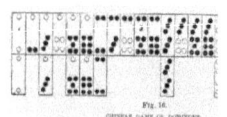
Sketch of dominoes from Stewart Culin's "Chinese Games with Dice and Dominoes." (Drawing by Stewart Culin, 1893)

# Placing a Bet

Chinese workers on the Canadian Pacific Railway gambling under a makeshift tent. While taken in 1886, almost two decades after the construction of the CPRR, this image shows how railroad workers, who carried few belongings with them, made use of locally available materials to construct a gambling table and tent. (Royal British Columbia Museum, B-09758, 193501-001)

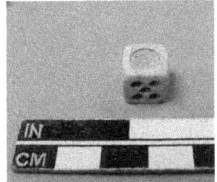

A Chinese die made of bone from Boise's Chinatown, excavated in 1979. This site dates from the late 1880s to the late 1920s. A die such as this was small and portable, and could have easily been carried in a railroad-worker's pocket. (Asian American Comparative Collection, University of Idaho, Moscow, 10AA146, 79-56, 4828-4829, 2015)

# Portable Games

Stock photo of *weiqi* board. Railroad workers could have easily created their own *weiqi* board by drawing lines in the ground using a stick.

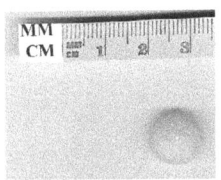

Photo of *weiqi* piece from Thompson River, the location of a Chinese construction camp for the Northern Pacific Railroad. (Photo by Gary Weisz, 2014)

Two Chinese *wen* from a Chinese construction camp for the Northern Pacific Railroad at Cabinet Landing, Idaho. (Photo by Gary Weisz, 2014)

Opium cans cut into gaming pieces found at Perma Bridge, an NPRR construction camp in Montana. (Photo by Sarah Armstrong Bard, 2014)

# Enjoying a Smoke

Fragments of kaolin pipe stems from the Northern Pacific Railroad construction camp along Twin Creek. (Photo by Gary Weisz, 2014)

Chinese tobacco pipe from the Carlin, Nevada, Chinese cemetery. (Courtesy of Sue Fawn Chung and John Joseph Crandall, 2014)

# Wine and Whiskey

Two Chinese liquor-bottle fragments in sand near railroad tie, Utah. (Photo by Chris Merritt, Utah Division of State History, 2015)

Base of Chinese liquor bottle from an archaeological site in Folsom, showing a mark. Liquor-bottle fragments have been found at many Chinese railroad sites. (Photo by PAR Environmental Services, Inc., 2011)

## Wine and Whiskey (continued)

Sketch of a porcelain decanter decorated in the Simple Flower motif. Fragments of similar vessels have been found at Denton Slough, a construction camp along the Northern Pacific Railroad in Idaho. (California State Parks and Recreation, 1984)

Small porcelain cup decorated in the Four Season Flower pattern from Folsom. Fragments of these small cups have been found at Lakeview Camp, a Chinese railroad camp near Carson City, Nevada. (Photo by PAR Environmental Services, Inc., 2014)

Neck and lip of a European or American liquor bottle found at the China Kitchen site in the Tahoe National Forest. (Photo by John Molenda, 2015)

# 6. Leaving a Legacy

## Divider

Cemetery of overseas Chinese workers whose remains were sent back to Guandong for burial. (Photo by Connie Young Yu, 2014)

## The Ten-Mile Day

Laying of last spike at Promontory Point. (Photo by Andrew Russell, 1869)

Cover illustration for the timetable and map of the Union & Central Pacific Railroad line, after about 1881.

"10 MILES OF TRACK, LAID IN ONE DAY. APRIL 28TH 1869." (Library of Congress online catalog)

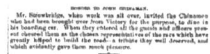

Image of newspaper article that details what was intended to be a separate ceremony of accomplishment held for Chinese railroad workers. The news articles did not list individual workers' names. (*San Francisco Newsletter*, May 15, 1869)

## Golden Spike National Historic Park

Site 42BO1134, Utah, near Promontory Point, Golden Spike National Historic Park. (Photo by Heather Weymouth, 2002)

Artifacts from 42BO1134, Utah, in Golden Spike National Historic Park. (Photo by Heather Weymouth, 2002)

# History Silenced

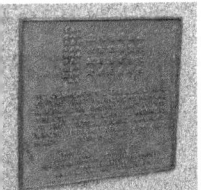

"TO COMMEMORATE THE CENTENNIAL OF THE FIRST TRANSCONTINENTAL RAILROAD IN AMERICA AND TO PAY TRIBUTE TO THE CHINESE WORKERS OF THE CENTRAL PACIFIC RAILROAD WHOSE INDOMITABLE COURAGE MADE IT POSSIBLE."(Plaque placed by the Chinese Historical Society of America, 1969)

# A Heritage of Discrimination

On March 8, 1887, San Jose City Council officials ordered the destruction of the Market Street Chinatown on the grounds that it was a health hazard to the surrounding area. Before the council edict could be enacted, an arson fire broke out on May 4, 1887, destroying the entire Chinatown. (History San Jose, 1887)

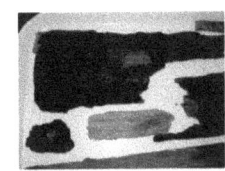

Fragments of wood and ceramics recovered from the Market Street Chinatown archaeological site show evidence of the town's burning. (Photos courtesy of Barbara L. Voss, 2012)

# Archaeology and Preservation of Memory

Archaeologists recording a hearth feature at Summit Camp site. (Photo by R. Scott Baxter, 2007)

Artifacts on the surface of the Summit Camp site. (Photo by Chris McClellan, 2014)

# Message on a Cliff Face in Montana

Close-up view of a Chinese inscription on the rock wall. It reads, "Sun Ziqian was here August 29."(Photos by Timothy R. Urbaniak, 1999)

Thousands of Chinese laborers worked and lived in camps like this while constructing transcontinental railways throughout the American West, but few historical images of such camps survive. This artistic rendition was created by integrating historical records and archaeological evidence to present a snapshot of work and life in the "Last Chance" Northern Pacific Railroad line camp along the Clark Fork River in northwestern Montana. (Courtesy of Eric Carlson, 2012)

## Old Ties and New Home Bases

Chinese New Year's Day in Chinatown, San Francisco, photographed between 1896 and 1906. (Photo by Arnold Genthe, Library of Congress LC-G4085-0198)

San Francisco Chinatown entryway. (Photo by Camille Majors, 2016)

This folk song is cited from *The Chinese Family Album* by Dorothy and Thomas Hoobler, 1994.

## Descendant Voices

Sunning Railroad in China, late 19th century. (Photo courtesy of Connie Young Yu, who was given the undated photo by Pearl Shew Lee)

## Chinese Railroad Workers in North America Project

Cover of thematic issue of *Historical Archaeology* 49(1), 2015: *The Archaeology of Chinese Railroad Workers in North America.*

## CHSA Dedication to the Chinese Railroad-Worker Legacy

Logo from the online exhibit of the Chinese Historical Society of America, at http://chsa.org/exhibits/online-exhibits/work-of-giants-the-chinese-and-the-building-of-the-first-transcontinental-railroad/.

Cover of *Voices of the Railroad: Stories by Descendants of Chinese Railroad Workers*, published by the Chinese Historical Society of America, 2014.

## 7. Appendices

## Divider

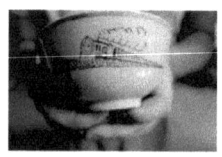

Ceramic bowl photographed in China. (Photo by Connie Young Yu, 2014)

# Timeline

| | |
|---|---|
| 1844 | United States acquired trading privileges with China through the Treaty of Wang Hya. |
| 1849 | California Gold Rush began. |
| 1854 | California Supreme Court decision in *People v. Hall* determined that Chinese people were not legally "white" and could not testify against "whites" in courts of law. |
| 1858 | California passed law to bar immigration of Chinese and other "Mongolians." |
| June 15, 1858 | The *Sacramento Union* reported on the hiring of 50 Chinese workers for the California Central Railroad, which "bids fair to demonstrate that Chinese laborers can be profitably employed in grading railroads in California." |
| 1860 | Sacramento merchant Collis P. Huntington agreed to invest in engineer Theodore Judah's railroad project and brought in four other investors: Mark Hopkins, James Bailey, Charles Crocker, and Leland Stanford. Together, they formed the first board of directors for the Central Pacific Railroad Company. |
| 1862 | Chinese Six Company formed through the federation of district associations. |
| July 1, 1862 | Congress passed the Pacific Railroad Bill that approved the Central Pacific project building the line from California, and chartered the Union Pacific Railroad Company to build westward from the Missouri River. |
| January 8, 1863 | In the groundbreaking ceremony at Sacramento, California, Governor Leland Stanford shoveled the first load of soil. |
| October 26, 1863 | The Central Pacific Railroad began work. |
| December 2, 1863 | The Union Pacific Railroad broke ground in Omaha, Nebraska. |
| January 1864 | The first recorded Chinese workers for the Central Pacific Railroad Company arrived. Foreman Ah Toy and headman Hung Wah led a crew of 21 men to work on clearing the Dutch Flat to Donner Lake Wagon Road. |
| January 20, 1865 | On the recommendation of his brother, E. B. Crocker, contractor Charles Crocker convinced foreman James Harvey Strobridge to look to Chinese employment to enlarge the overall labor pool. |
| Summer 1865 | Track was completed across Newcastle Gap and work began on Clipper Gap, 43 miles from Sacramento, at the base of Cape Horn. This was another major section of the railroad and would take a year to grade and track. In July 1865, the Central Pacific Railroad imported the first large group of Chinese from China. |
| Fall 1865 | Work began building 13 tunnels through the Sierra Nevada. Chinese laborers working in three shifts around the clock undertook construction of Summit Tunnel No. 6. This tunnel would be the longest at 1,659 ft. and up to 124 ft. below the surface. On November 21, the *Sacramento Union* reported that approximately 4,000 men, "mostly Chinese," were at work on the Central Pacific. |
| July 1866 | The rail line to Dutch Flat, 69 miles from Sacramento, was completed. The Chinese workforce was at approximately 3,933. |
| Winter 1866-1867 | One of the harshest winters in California history struck, featuring 44 storms and averaging 18 ft. of snow at the summit. Despite this, the Chinese workers continued work on the tunnels. By this time, the Tunnel No. 6 labor force was almost completely composed of Chinese workers. Avalanches posed particular danger, as demonstrated at Strong's Canyon (Tunnels Nos. 11 and 12), known as Camp No. 4, which included two gangs of Chinese and a gang of culvert men. |

| | |
|---|---|
| *February 1867* | The Chinese workforce was made up of approximately 8,000 men on the tunnels and 3,000 laying track east of Cisco, 92 miles east of Sacramento. |
| *June 1867* | Several thousand Chinese went on strike for a pay increase from $35 to $40 per month and a reduced workday of eight hours. On June 30, the *Daily Alta California* reported on the strike that began the previous Tuesday (June 25). The Chinese strikers' demands were reported in the *San Francisco Dispatch*, July 1, 1867, and the Boston *Daily Evening Voice*, August 5, 1867. The strike lasted about a week, during which management, headed by Crocker and Strobridge, halted food-supply trains to starve out the workers. In the end, the strike was not successful. On July 3, the *Daily Alta* relayed Charles Crocker's report that, with the exception of one or two gangs, all Chinese resumed working with no change in pay. |
| *August 1867* | A year after the vertical shaft for the Summit Tunnel had been drilled, workers broke through to complete the project. Tunnel No. 6 measured 1,659 ft. in length, and 124 ft. deep into the rock. |
| *October 31, 1867* | The *Daily Alta California* reported that approximately 8,000 of the 50,000 Chinese in California were currently employed on the Pacific Railroad. |
| *1868* | The Burlingame Treaty between the U.S. and China granted federal recognition for Chinese travel to the U.S. as visitors, traders, or permanent residents. |
| *April 1868* | The Central Oregon Railroad had a Chinese crew on hand and projected the hiring of an additional 1,000 Chinese laborers. |
| *May 1868* | The rail line from Truckee to Reno was completed. On May 1, the *San Francisco Bulletin* reported from the Portland *Oregonian* that Superintendent Hart of the Oregon Central Railroad and his contractors employed 40 Chinese and expected in the next day or two to employ 25 or so more. The grading was progressing at a rate of two miles per week. |
| *February 22, 1869* | The Salt Lake *Telegraph* reported (and the *Sacramento Union* re-published) that the Sierra region had a great snowstorm that caused a blockade for the railroads. The storm was the worst of the winter, but the Union Pacific and Central Pacific crews continued to move closer toward each other. Union Pacific Irish workers allegedly "shake the bland persistence of the Chinese by jeering and by tossing frozen clods at them. When those tactics had no restraining effect, they staged sudden raids with pick handles." When the Chinese "fought back with unexpected vigor and accuracy," the Irish also set off heavy powder charges "when the closest part of the C. P. grade was swarming with Chinese. As a result, several Chinese were critically hurt." After the Central Pacific complained, the Union Pacific ordered its men to stop. |
| *April 28, 1869* | The Central Pacific, with teams of mostly Chinese workers and some Irish workers, set a record by laying 10 miles and 56 feet of track in 12 hours at Rozel, Utah. The effort was sparked by a competitive bet with the Union Pacific, whose men had once laid 7 miles of track in one stretch (but they had reportedly worked from four in the morning until midnight, beyond a regular day's work). The *San Francisco Bulletin* called the feat "the greatest work in tracklaying ever accomplished or conceived by railroad men." A top-ranking army commander, who was watching the workers' progress with his soldiers, said: "Mr. Crocker, I never saw such organization as that. It was just like an army marching over the ground and leaving the track built behind them." |
| *May 10, 1869* | The word "DONE" was telegraphed to Washington, D.C., and the transcontinental railroad was officially completed. Some Chinese workmen reportedly had to finish putting in the iron spikes that pinned the rails to the tie; promptly afterward the tie "was attacked by hundreds of jack-knives, and soon reduced to a mere stick." Several Chinese, including the foreman Hung Wah, were invited by Superintendent Strobridge to a reception held in his private car with press and officers of the 21st Regiment, where they "were his honored guests and were cheered as they entered." Despite these singularities, the Chinese were largely kept absent from the publicized event, although *Harper's Monthly Magazine*'s history of the transcontinental railroad claims that "coolies from San Francisco" were present. The workers moved on to other projects, including other railroads in California, along the West Coast, and in the South, or became farmers. |

| | |
|---|---|
| November 10, 1869 | The Houston & Texas Central Railroad's agent, John B. Walker, signed a contract with San Francisco labor contractor Chew Ah Heang for 300 workers. |
| 1870 | The Federal Civil Rights Act voided the California's Foreign Miners' License Tax and Chinese Capitation Tax and extended contract-law rights and court-proceeding rights to Chinese immigrants. |
| April 1870 | Approximately 300 Chinese passed through Reno, Nevada, on their way to build a railroad in Nevada. |
| Summer 1870 | The Houston & Texas Central Railroad discharged most of its Chinese workers due to hostility from Irish fellow workers and financial constraints. Most of the Chinese laborers stayed in Texas, some going to work on farms. |
| Winter 1870 | The Alabama Chattanooga Railroad employed between 600 and 700 Chinese workers. |
| December 28, 1870 | Up to 300 Chinese from California arrived in St. Louis, Missouri, bound for Texas, according to the *St. Louis Democrat* on December 30. According to the *Galveston Civilian*, the Chinese were formerly workers on the Central Pacific Railroad and would go on to work on the Texas Railroad in a test run of the southern plan. They left California by train and first arrived in Council Bluffs, Iowa, before reaching St Louis. |
| 1871 | The Walla Walla & Columbia River Railroad contracted Chinese laborers to work on the construction of the line from Walla Walla to Wallula, Washington. This route was completed in 1875. |
| 1872 | By this time, approximately 1,500 Chinese workers were working on railways and telegraph lines in Oregon. According to the *New Northwest*, "near Lake Pend d'Oreille in northeast Washington, 1,800 Chinese and 900 white laborers worked together without tension or incidents." Chinese laborers also worked on railroads in Whitman, Spokane, and Stevens counties in Washington. |
| January 1873 | Journalist Charles Nordhoff published his book, *California: For Health, Pleasure, and Residence,* which included a chapter on his 1870 observations of the Chinese working on a Central Pacific Railroad job in Merced (with Strobridge as "contractor"). Nordhoff described their wages, working conditions, and their food, imported from China and of which the Chinese "have a greater variety ... than their white neighbors" and "live ... far better." |
| 1875 | Federal Page Law prohibited immigration of Chinese, Japanese, and "Mongolian" prostitutes, felons, and contract laborers. |
| March 1875 | More than 330 Chinese tunnel diggers worked on the Southern Pacific Railroad line to Los Angeles. The crew bored the 6,975 ft. long San Fernando Tunnel, the longest west of the Appalachians. The force included at least 1,000 Chinese among the 1,500-person crew. |
| June 4, 1879 | *Frank Leslie's Illustrated Newspaper* reported 6,000 Chinese laborers began work on the Texas Pacific Railroad. |
| 1880 | U.S. and China signed a treaty that gave the U.S. the right to limit Chinese immigration. |
| 1880s | The Northern Pacific Railroad, a transcontinental railroad through Washington, Idaho, and Montana, hired up to 15,000 Chinese railroad workers. The Northern Pacific Railroad "Golden Spike" was driven in 1883 in Montana, but the railway continued west. |
| May 1881 | The Southern Pacific Railroad reached El Paso, Texas, from Los Angeles. The majority of the Southern Pacific Railroad workforce was Chinese (about 2,600 out of roughly 3,000). Under their supervisor, J. H. Strobridge, former superintendent for the Central Pacific Railroad, the Chinese were reportedly "treated more like slaves," according to the *San Antonio Light*. |
| 1882 | Chinese Exclusion Act prohibited the entry of Chinese laborers for period of 10 years, allowing only merchants and professionals; wives and children of Chinese laborers were also prohibited. |
| 1888 | Scott Act limited the re-entry of Chinese immigrants. |
| 1892 | Geary Act extended the Chinese Exclusion Act for 10 additional years and required Chinese residents of the U.S. to register with local authorities and carry certificates of lawful residence. |

| | |
|---|---|
| *1902* | Chinese Exclusion Act was renewed for 10 more years. |
| *1904* | Chinese Exclusion Act was made indefinite. |
| *1905* | Transnational Chinese boycott of U.S.–made products began to protest the U.S. government's treatment of Chinese immigrants. |
| *1906* | San Francisco earthquake destroyed municipal and immigration records, and created opportunities for Chinese claims to U.S. citizenship, resulting in increased immigration. |
| *1911* | China Republican Revolution in China ended Qing dynasty rule. |
| *1919* | On May 10, Chinese railroad workers Ging Cui, Wong Fook, and Lee Shao were invited to stand on the float during a celebration of the Golden Spike 50th Anniversary held in Ogden, Utah. |
| *1922* | Cable Act provided that any United States female citizen who married an alien ineligible for citizenship forfeited her own citizenship. |
| *1924* | National Origins Act closed immigration from all Asian countries and included the family members of U.S. citizens of Asian descent. |
| *1939* | A celebration was held in Omaha, Nebraska, to celebrate the joining of the Union Pacific and CPRR rails. The highlight of the celebration was the viewing of Cecil B. DeMille's *Union Pacific*, a film that featured a re-enactment of Stanford's driving the Golden Spike, purportedly using the original Golden Spike as a film prop. |
| *1941* | Pearl Harbor Attack caused the U.S. and China to enter into a military alliance against Japan. |
| *1943* | Chinese Exclusion Repeal Act passed; it instituted a quota of 105 Chinese immigrants per year and granted the right of naturalized citizenship to Chinese immigrants. |
| *1944* | The U.S. Post Office issued a commemorative stamp celebrating the 75th anniversary of the joining of the Central Pacific and Union railroads. |
| *1947* | War Brides Act Amendment allowed thousands of Chinese American U.S. servicemen to bring their wives and children to the U.S. from China. |
| *1965-1969* | Golden Spike National Historic Site was created in Utah. Chinese were excluded from the main ceremony of 1969. |
| *2009* | Colfax Historical Society in California sponsored the placing of California historical markers along the railroad route. |
| *May 10, 2012* | Event at Golden Spike National Historic Site, with the recreation of the famous Russell photograph. Many photographs were taken with Chinese descendants of railroad workers and visitors from Guangdong, China. |
| *September 2012* | Stanford University launched the Chinese Railroad Workers in North American Project, http://web.stanford.edu/group/chineserailroad/cgi-bin/wordpress/. |
| *October 10-12, 2013* | Archaeology Workshop of the Chinese Railroad Workers in North America Project occurred. |
| *May 9, 2014* | U.S. Department of Labor inducted Chinese transcontinental-railroad workers into the Hall of Honor. |

# For Further Reading

Asian American Comparative Collection
2015   http://webpages.uidaho.edu/aacc/.

Bailey, William F.
1908   The Story of the Central Pacific. The Rise of the Big Four: Huntington, Stanford, Crocker, and
       Hopkins. *Pacific Monthly* 20(1). Central Pacific Railroad Photographic History Museum,
       http://cprr.org/Museum/Bailey_CPRR_1908.html.

Baxter, R. Scott
2008   The Response of California's Chinese Population to the Anti-Chinese Movement. *Historical
       Archaeology* 42(3):29–36.

Central Pacific Railroad Photographic History Museum
2015   http://www.cprr.org/.

Central Pacific Railroad Photographic History Museum
2015   Pottery Relics Used in 19th Century Central Pacific Railroad Chinese Workers Camps.
       http://cprr.org/Museum/Ephemera/CPRR_Chinese_Pottery.html.

Chew, William F.
2004   *Nameless Builders of the Transcontinental*. Trafford Publishing, Victoria, BC.

Chinese in Northwest American Research Committee
2015   http://www.cinarc.org.

Chinese Historical Society of America
2015   Work of Giants: Chinese Railroad Worker Project.
       http://chsa.org/2015/07/work-of-giants-chinese-railroad-worker-project/.

Chinese Railroad Workers in North America Project, Stanford University
2015   http://web.stanford.edu/group/chineserailroad/cgi-bin/wordpress/.

Choy, Philip P.
2014   Interpreting "Overseas Chinese" Ceramics. Society for Historical Archaeology, Research Resource,
       http://sha.org/resources/chinese-ceramics/.

Culin, Stewart
1891   The Gambling Games of the Chinese in America. *Series in Philology Literature and Archeology*
       1(4):1–18. Internet Archive, http://www.archive.org/details.gamblinggamessch01culigoog.

Culin, Stewart
1895   Chinese Games with Dice and Dominoes. *Report of the U.S. National Museum for 1893*, pp. 489–
       537. Internet Archive, http://www.archive.org/details/chinesegameswith01culi.

Fan, Warner J. W.
1996   *A Manual of Chinese Herbal Medicine: Principles and Practice for Easy Reference*. Shambhala,
       Boston, MA.

Greenwood, Roberta S.
1996    *Down by the Station. Los Angeles Chinatown 1880–1933.* University of California, Berkeley, Institute of Archaeology, Monumenta Archaeologica 18.

Heath, Erle
1927    From Trail to Rail. A History of the Southern Pacific Railroad Company. *Bulletin* 7:11–12. Central Pacific Railroad Photographic History Museum, http://cprr.org/Museum/Southern_Pacific_Bulletin/index.html.

Kraus, George
1969    Chinese Laborers and the Construction of the Central Pacific. *Utah Historical Quarterly* 37(1):41–57. Central Pacific Railroad Photographic History Museum, http://cprr.org/Museum/Last_Spike_is_Driven.pdf.

Lee, Sue, and Connie Young Yu (editors)
2014    *Voices from the Railroad: Stories by Descendants of Chinese Railroad Workers.* Chinese Historical Society of America, San Francisco, CA.

Reid, Daniel P.
1993    *Chinese Herbal Medicine.* Shambhala, Boston, MA.

Richardson, Abby
1871    Garnered Sheaves: From the Writings of Albert P. Richardson. Columbian Book Company, Hartford, CT. Central Pacific Railroad Photographic History Museum, http://cprr.org/Museum/Through_to_the_Pacific/Through_to_the_Pacific.html.

Richardson, Albert P.
1869    Through to the Pacific (A Series of Letters). *New York Tribune*, May–June. Central Pacific Railroad Photographic History Museum, http://cprr.org/Museum/Through_to_the_Pacific/Through_to_the_Pacific.html.

Schulz, Peter D., and Rebecca Allen (compilers)
2008    Archaeology and Architecture of the Overseas Chinese: A Bibliography. *Historical Archaeology* 42(3):171–193. Society for Historial Archaeology, https://sha.org/assets/documents/research/Bibliography/arch_artchit_chinese_biblio.pdf.

University of Michigan Digital Library
2014    http://www.lib.umich.edu/digital-library-production-service-dlps.
        Links to books at the University of Michigan relating to the transcontinental railroad also at Central Pacific Railroad Photographic History Museum, http://cprr.org/Museum/Books/Books%20Online.html.

Voss, Barbara L. (editor)
2015    *The Archaeology of Chinese Railroad Workers in North America.* Thematic issue, *Historical Archaeology* 49(1).

Voss, Barbara L., and Rebecca Allen
2008    Overseas Chinese Archaeology: Historical Foundations, Current Reflections, and New Directors. *Historical Archaeology* 42(3):5–28.

Wegars, Priscilla S. (editor)
1993    *Hidden Heritage: Historical Archaeology of the Overseas Chinese.* Baywood Publishing, Amityville, NY.

# *Acknowledgments*

In October 2013, the Chinese Railroad Workers in North America Project hosted a workshop at the Stanford Archaeology Center (Stanford University). The workshop's purpose was to provide a forum for collaboration among archaeologists and interested historians, artists, authors, community activists, researchers, and preservation planners. The tone of the workshop was scholarly. The workshop's organizer, Dr. Barbara L. Voss, asked this primary research question: "In the absence of direct written evidence from the workers themselves, could archaeology be used to reconstruct the historical experience of Chinese laborers who built the first transcontinental and many of the other railroads in the American West?" The answer was a resounding "YES," and archaeologists and other researchers began talking to one another. This volume was born out of the desire to take this message and present it to a wider audience, one that was very interested in the historical past, but not part of the professional archaeological network.

All three of this volume's primary authors are committed to interpreting the past in ways that make it more relevant to the present and accessible to the public. We recognize that not only are scholarship and the careful choice of words critical to this process, but that visual images often carry the message in ways that words cannot express. In creating this volume, we had a lot of assistance and are grateful to a number of individuals and institutions.

From the Chinese Railroad Workers in North America Project, we would like to thank Professors Gordon Chang, Shelley Fisher Fishkin, and Barbara L. Voss. We have also had the assistance of Gabriel Wolfenstein, Hilton Obenzinger, and others. From the Chinese Historical Society of America, Sue Lee and Connie Young lent their voices and unique perspectives on Chinese railroad-worker descendants.

Environmental Science Associates donated time for Rebecca Allen to write the text and find the right photographs and illustrations. R. Scott Baxter also helped with the photo hunt. Camille Majors and an ESA team of graphic artists took our rough layouts and vision for this volume and turned them into the product before you, not an easy task, but always handled with humor and professionalism.

PAR Environmental Services, Inc., sponsored time for Amber Rankin, Sarah Heffner, and Mary Maniery. Amber Rankin, PAR's graphics specialist, devoted countless hours creating images of Chinese laborers and interpreting historical photographs and our verbal descriptions of camp life in illustrations meant to appeal to the general public. She displayed incredible patience working through countless edits and minute changes and is thanked for her insights and effort.

From the Society for Historical Archaeology, Richard Schaefer provided expert copy editing. Working with him is always a delight. Annalies Corbin, SHA Publications Editor, and Ruth Perry of the PAST Foundation provided a pathway to publication.

We would also like to thank our guest authors: Chris Merritt, Michael Polk, Kelly Dixon, Timothy Urbaniak, Sue Fawn Chung, and John Joseph Crandall. Others lent us their photographs, site maps, and artifact sketches: Adrianna Allen, Sarah Armstrong Bard, G. J. "Chris" Graves, Clement Lai, Chris McClellan, John Molenda, Gary Weisz, Paul Chace, Julia Costello, Tammara Norton, Scott Baxter, Sharon Waechter, and Kenneth Cannon.

Finally, we would like to thank our families, friends, and colleagues who read our drafts, listened to our thoughts, and brainstormed with us to develop the subject matter, artifact list, and overall volume.

www.ingramcontent.com/pod-product-compliance
Lightning Source LLC
Chambersburg PA
CBHW041118120626
46547CB00019B/2763